*Spanish Film under Franco*

# Spanish Film under Franco

Virginia Higginbotham

 University of Texas Press, Austin

Publication of this work has been made possible in part by a grant from the Program for Cultural Cooperation between Spain's Ministry of Culture and United States Universities.

Some material in this book previously appeared in "Spanish film under Franco: Do Not Disturb," by Virginia Higginbotham, originally published in WORLD CINEMA SINCE 1945 edited by William H. Luhr. Copyright © 1987 by The Ungar Publishing Company. Reprinted by permission of the publisher.

Photographs from films directed by Carlos Saura courtesy of Producciones Querejeta, Madrid. Photographs from all other films courtesy of Filmoteca Nacional, Madrid.

First edition, 1988

Requests for permission to reproduce material from this work should be sent to:
    Permissions
    University of Texas Press
    Box 7819
    Austin, Texas 78713-7819

LIBRARY OF CONGRESS CATALOGING-IN-PUBLICATION DATA

Higginbotham, Virginia, 1935–
    Spanish film under Franco / Virginia Higginbotham.—1st
ed.
      p.    cm.
    Filmography: p.
    Bibliography: p.
    Includes index.
    1. Moving-pictures—Spain—History.  2. Moving-
pictures—Censorship—Spain.  3. Moving-pictures—Political
aspects—Spain.  4. Spain—Politics and government—
1939–1975.  I. Title.
PN1993.5.S7H54   1988
791'.43'0946—dc 19                 87-15649
                                           CIP

ISBN: 978-0-292-77603-6

# Contents

# Illustrations

# Preface

The cinema of almost every European country has been described in countless books on British, Italian, French, and German film. Yet, for nearly a decade, the only discussion of Spanish film in English has been Vicente Molina-Foix's excellent forty-seven-page *New Cinema in Spain*, published in London in 1977. Now, film critics are trying to catch up. Peter Besas's recent survey of Spanish film in *Behind the Spanish Lens* is complemented by Ronald Schwartz's informative *Spanish Film Directors, 1950–1985*. With these authors' emphasis on film directors, however, there is still no full-length critical analysis in English of Spanish cinema. *Spanish Film under Franco* is intended to fill this surprising void. Although not a comprehensive history, it provides a historical perspective of Spanish film during the Franco era as a background for analysis of the major works of Spanish cinema. *Spanish Film under Franco* analyzes film both as a national art form and as a form of national discourse on prominent social and political issues. Thus films selected for analysis in the book are those of particular artistic value or that contribute significantly to the national dialogue.

*Spanish Film under Franco* begins with a brief overview of prewar film in Spain. By 1936, three directors of enormous talent—Luis Buñuel, the documentarist, Carlos Velo, and Luis Alcoriza—were working in Spain's film industry. At the outbreak of the Spanish Civil War in July 1936 they emigrated, all eventually to Mexico, where each gained international recognition for films they made there. During the Civil War the Spanish film industry established a technical and distribution network capable of being readily transformed by the two opposing sides into production of newsreels and war documentaries.

During the Franco era leading Spanish film historians such as Carlos Fernández Cuenca[1] and Fernando Vizcaíno Casas[2] insisted that after the Civil War Spain had no "official" political cinema. In truth, there was little else. Such a denial could only be made by upholders of what Roland

Barthes describes in *Mythologies* as a myth that has already achieved the state of appearing to be a natural order, a status quo.

Barthes's conception of myth as a second-order semiological system, a system of meaning defined by its intention rather than by its literal sense, helps to illuminate the language of a cinema which attempts to portray history, as did Spanish film under Franco. For myth, Barthes observes, "deprives the object of which it speaks all history."[3] Thus history transformed into myth becomes distorted and duplicitous in order to serve not fact, or authenticity, or even the demands of the box office, but an intention. Franco's intention, of course, was to force acceptance of his military dictatorship, and he used film as a visual language to impose the mythology of his regime. My book is not a methodical semiological study but refers to Barthes's theory of myth, that fragment of semiology, as it enhances understanding of the rhetoric and censorship of Spanish film under Franco.

Chapter 2 describes the thorough and relentless film censorship of the Franco era. Modeled on Mussolini's example, it lasted longer than anywhere else in Western Europe. All opposition voices were banned, which meant that no newsreels, documentaries, or fiction films seeming to favor ideas opposed by the regime were seen by the public. During the 1950s, the only genres acceptable to the Franco government, described in Chapter 3, were war epics and historical extravaganzas celebrating the glories of Spain's colonial past in images of patriotism, militarism, and religious heroism; that is, the same values held by those who won the Spanish Civil War.

Censorship under Franco lasted so long and was so rigid that young filmmakers who wanted to comment in their works on current life in Spain or express opinions critical of the regime were forced to develop a countermyth whose highly metaphorical and convoluted syntax, known as the *estética franquista* (Francoist aesthetic), was not immediately decipherable by censors. Juan Antonio Bardem and Luis Berlanga, founders of post–Civil War Spanish film, began to devise a cinema of countermyth in the 1950s and 1960s which, in order to subvert censorship, conveyed their ideas indirectly by subtle analogy, pastiche, allusion, and inference. Their works are discussed in Chapters 4 and 5.

In 1960, the Franco regime, in an effort to appear democratic in the eyes of Europeans, whose economic Common Market it aspired to enter, began to relax censorship of foreign films. New opportunities were also offered to young Spanish directors. With the opening of a system of art theaters as well as the national film archives, Spain at last seemed to nourish a national film culture. Chapter 6 describes the changes in Spanish cinema resulting from *apertura*, or thaw, in international relations.

Luis Buñuel's films had been banned by the more liberal Republicans before the Civil War. They were anathema to Franco, who continued the ban against them and even prohibited mention of the director's name in film dictionaries. In 1960, however, as a part of *apertura,* Buñuel was invited to return to his homeland and make a film. The result was *l'affaire Viridiana,* which heaped international ridicule upon the Franco government and accolades upon Buñuel, who had made his career subverting censorship and satirizing society. The incident brought Buñuel instant recognition in Spain, where few had seen his films, and made him a living myth among students and filmmakers there. Buñuel's impact is nowhere more evident than in the films of the young Carlos Saura.

Saura was one of a number of young directors known collectively as the "New Spanish Cinema" whose chance to make films was a result of *apertura.* He not only refined the *estética franquista* devised by Berlanga and Bardem, but enriched it with surrealist allusions borrowed from Buñuel. Like Buñuel, whom Saura refers to as his "spiritual father," the young rebel scandalized Spaniards with the political allegories for which he has won acclaim. Films such as *La caza (The Hunt)* and *La prima Angelica (Cousin Angelica)* won favorable reviews from American critics when screened in the United States. In Spain, however, they stirred angry dialogue and opened old wounds. As in the case of Buñuel, Saura's films would not have been heard of in Spain had they not won prizes and praise from foreign audiences who viewed them at film festivals abroad. Because he was able to work consistently and thus elaborate a personal film language and vision, Saura's films are discussed separately in Chapter 8.

Others of the New Spanish Cinema were not so fortunate. The crack in the fascist façade closed in 1969, thus revealing its true character as a public relations display for the purpose of creating a civilized image of the Franco government. Sealed back into oblivion were the hopes of young directors, many of whom were only able to make one film before their sole points of distribution within Spain—the art theaters—were closed and their films left without an audience in their own country. Some of these directors, whose works are described in Chapter 9, became embittered and abandoned filmmaking after their first effort.

Those who were allowed to continue, such as producer Elías Querejeta and Carlos Saura, were perceived by many of their colleagues as tools of the Franco regime. Saura, merely by working in Franco's Spain, was considered by some as the *hombre bufón* (buffoon) of Spanish film.[4] Yet the works of these young directors, including Angelino Fons's *La busca (The Search),* Miguel Picazo's *La tía Tula (Aunt Tula),* and Victor Erice's *El espíritu de la colmena (Spirit of the Beehive),* are eloquent testimony to their determination to resist the social and political myths imposed by the Franco dictatorship.

In the decade since Franco's death on November 20, 1975, Spain has undergone transition from almost a half-century of dictatorship to modern democratic monarchy. Change has not come easily for Spain. Under close scrutiny by its European neighbors and American allies, it emerged from the long dictatorship still not economically and socially integrated into the twentieth century. Divorce laws, rescinded by Franco, had to be reinstated. Laws making women equal rather than subservient to their husbands were also passed. As late as 1961 women could be fired from their jobs when they married—an attempt by the regime to keep women at home to raise large families.[5] The right to strike and to hold demonstrations, as well as basic freedoms of speech and press, had to be rewoven into the legal fabric of Spanish society. Spain's first elections in over forty years were held in 1977.

Spanish cinema of the transition period, relatively free of the constrictions which had oppressed it for half its lifetime, released an initial burst of political satire. Gonzálo Herralde takes aim at Franco in *Raza, el espíritu de Franco,* a compilation documentary of the dictator's life based on a series of interviews. Basilio Martín Patino also compiles an ironic view of the dictator in *Caudillo,* using documentary footage from the archives of Lisbon and London. Jaime Chávarri reveals the decay of post–Civil War values in *El desencanto (Disenchantment),* a collection of filmed interviews with the family of Leopoldo Panero, a poet who sang the virtues of Franco.

Although censorship has subsided, transition filmmakers are still wary after forty years of repression. The climate of the post–Franco years, punctuated by frequent rumors of and an attempt (November 1978) at an army coup, is more relaxed, but the *estética franquista* remains a predominant film style. José Luis Garcia Sánchez, who says he feels he was born on November 20, 1975, directed the scathing but very oblique and bitter *Las truchas (The Trout),* which describes middle-class conformity and capitulation to power. Manuel Gutiérrez Aragón, who worked on the script of *Las truchas,* directed his own allegory, *Camada negra (Black Brood),* a darkly comic satire of the Spanish family and of Spanish susceptibility to fascistic and militaristic rituals of behavior. Few of the young filmmakers have touched the experience of the Civil War. Coming closest to reopening this long-closed period of history is Josep María Forn's *Companys: Proceso a Cataluña,* an account of the final years of the leader of the Catalán government, Lluis Companys, and his assassination in 1940 by Franco supporters. After a brief glance into the recent past, however, Spanish cinema of the transition years has turned away to other, less demanding topics with more box office appeal.

Since the Second World War, innumerable fiction films and documentaries of combat, espionage, and intrigue have filled American and European screens with images of that war from every possible point of view.

The experiences of World War II and the inquiries into the fascist period of the 1930s and 1940s are so numerous as to constitute new film genres. Through such films, a significant historical event resonates in the minds of a public already a generation removed from it. In Spain, however, the defeat of half the country smoldered in the national psyche for almost half a century. As Barthes explains, history evaporates in myth; thus, Spanish cinema has so far filmed only oblique, sporadic compilations of the experience of the Civil War. During the years of transition from dictatorship to democracy, Spanish filmmakers have only tentatively begun to probe their country's past, to undertake a cinematic inquiry into their nation's recent history.

This book arose from necessity. While teaching courses on Hispanic film at the University of Texas, I discovered not only that adequate materials for study of Spanish film were lacking, but I also found students to be light years away from the culture depicted in the films they were being required to screen. Those who were eager to penetrate the mysteries of these texts had almost no sources outside a scattering of reviews in British and French film periodicals. No Spanish film periodicals reach our library.

So, with a grant from the University Research Institute, I went in search of materials in Madrid and Barcelona. Had I not gained prior access to information obtained by William McRae, who preceded me in gathering data at the Filmoteca Nacional in Madrid, I would have returned empty-handed; for there was, in the spring of 1982, still no list of films available to the public of the holdings of this national archive. The professional staff there, however, especially archives director Carlos Serrano de Osma, head librarian Dolores Devesa, and stills curator Miguel Soria, assisted me with consistent courtesy and good will. My study would have been impossible without them.

My understanding of Spanish film was expanded by conversations with two of Spain's best film critics, Román Gubern and José María Caparrós. Finally, my work in the Biblioteca Caralt in Barcelona, where I was assisted by Delmiro Caralt and his associate, Montserrat Bofill, enriched my life as well as the dimensions of my research. These two extraordinary people are quietly and almost single-handedly administering one of the most exciting and extensive film libraries anywhere. Their understanding, kindness, and eagerness to facilitate my work are among the rare gifts that I will never be able to repay.

*Spanish Film under Franco*

# 1. Introduction: Prewar Spanish Film

At the turn of the century, Spain was, as Vizcaíno Casas points out, culturally closer to Europe than it was at mid century.[1] Only five months after the Lumière brothers captured the world's imagination with the first moving pictures in December 1895, the Spanish were viewing them in Madrid. The Lumière representative, A. Promio, projected the first movies in Spain at the Hotel Rusia on May 11, 1896, to an audience which included the students of the College of San Luis de los Franceses and the French ambassador to Spain. Promio not only ran the historic footage but also shot the first films ever made in Spain. Following what appears to have been a Lumière tradition, this earliest segment was of young schoolgirls leaving class and was entitled *Salida de las alumnas del Colegio de San Luis de los Franceses (Students Coming Out of the College of San Luis of the French)*.

Buñuel's home province must have provided an especially fertile field for the new art. The first two Spaniards to go to Paris to acquire the "Lumière machine" were, like Buñuel, from Aragón—Eduardo Jimeno Junior and Senior, a father and son who operated a wax museum in Madrid. In making the first Spanish movies, they added a Spanish touch to the Lumière fascination with groups emerging from buildings with brief footage entitled *Salida de la misa de 12 de la Iglesia del Pilar en Zaragoza (Coming Out of Noon Mass at the Church of Pilar in Zaragoza)*. Although Zaragoza remained on the margin of film activity in Spain, it has the distinction of being the home of both Spain's first, as well as its most famous, film director. Luis Buñuel, born in nearby Calanda, spent his youth in the provincial capital of Zaragoza.

The most prolific and imaginative of the early Spanish filmmakers was a photography enthusiast from Gracia, then a suburb of Barcelona. Fructuoso Gelabert not only made his own camera but in 1898 shot a forty-meter documentary on the royal family's visit to Barcelona which he sold to the Pathé brothers in Paris. He added the Catalán spirit to Lumière's tradition of cinematic egress in two short segments: *Salida de los obreros de la España industrial* (*Workers Leaving Industrial Spain*) and *Salida de la Iglesia de Sans* (*Coming Out of the Sans Cathedral*). In addition to being the first Spanish documentarist, filming bicycle races and, inevitably, bullfights, Gelabert also made feature films such as *María Rosa* (1908), *La Dolores* (1908), and *Ana Kadova* (1912). He also directed a series of socially aware episodes, including *La España trágica* and *Las entrañas de Madrid* (*The Heart of Madrid*).

Some of the most significant contributions to Spanish cinema were made in the early days of its development. A modest engineer, also from Aragón, named Segundo de Chomón had a distinguished career as an inventor of techniques which provided the foundation of today's most advanced procedures. Born in Teruel in 1871, Chomón was descended from the ancient French family of Chaumont (it was in the French village of Chaumont, on the Upper Marne River, where Catherine de Medici had resided in the castle of Chaumont).[2] About 1900, Chomón became interested in the possibilities of color film. In his Barcelona laboratory he experimented with stencil tinting of each frame of short films. In 1906 he joined Pathé in Paris, where he worked with film coloring and developed further his interest in animation and special effects.

Chomón's most original animation was the 150-meter film *El hotel eléctrico* (*The Electric Hotel*), which he made in Barcelona. It is a kind of electric slapstick in miniature, in which a couple arrives at a hotel, elevators go up and down, doors open and close, and luggage moves about without being carried. Made in 1905, *El hotel eléctrico* precedes by two years American James Stuart Blackton's *The Haunted Hotel*, generally considered the earliest landmark in animation.

While at Pathé, in 1907, Chomón was the first to devise a moving camera for what is now known as the traveling or dolly shot. He did not perfect the technique, however, until after he had left Pathé to join Giovanni Pastrone in Turin, Italy, where he was hired to create special effects. Chomón, a meticulous and methodical worker, was too modest to patent his own inventions, so in 1912 the patent for the traveling shot was recorded in Pastrone's name.

In 1914, Chomón created special effects for *Cabiria*, considered an extravaganza in its time. For scenes of burning ships in the bay of Syracuse and the eruption of Etna, Chomón used three levels of superimposed images and filled the sails of model ships in the bay with blowing air. When Italian cinema began its post–World War I slump, Chomón returned to Paris and, in 1925, worked with Abel Gance on *Napoleon*.

As public preference seemed increasingly to favor realism over fantasy and tricks, the need for special effects faded and Chomón was out of work. He returned to Spain, but studios in Madrid and Barcelona were below the technical level of those in Paris. Chomón became ill while shooting a color film in Morocco for a Spanish company and died in May 1929. Since he had spent most of his career abroad, Chomón's contributions to cinema were almost unknown in Spain and were largely unrecognized there until the centenary celebration accorded him in 1971.

Largely through lack of capital, cinema in Spain before the Civil War did not fulfill the promise of its earliest pioneers. Its first thirty-six years, however, developed without the constraints and distortions of the postwar period. Themes of national life and customs were popular, and social problems were not, as later, prohibited from being examined on the screen. One of the best films of the prewar era was Florián Rey's *La aldea maldita* (*The Cursed Village*) (1929), which dealt with the plight of rural workers fleeing from a severe drought to urban areas in search of a better life. *Zalacaín el aventuerero* (*Zalacaín, the Adventurer*) (1930), adapted from Pío Baroja's novel by director Francisco Camacho, was another serious effort to examine political restlessness in rural villages. Divorce was presented favorably by Gómez Hidalgo in his amazing *La malcasada* (1926). For the first time, Spanish artists, politicians, journalists, even the young General Franco can be seen in the frames of a fiction film.[3] Joseph Bloy's *La España de hoy* (*Spain Today*) (1929) was a blatant praise of the progress made in Spain since the fall of dictator Primo de Rivera.

As in other countries, much of Spanish early cinema drew its themes from literature. In 1909, two of Spain's master plays, *Don Juan Tenorio* and *Los amantes de Teruel* (*The Lovers of Teruel*) were made into films. A steady stream of comedies was adapted from the farces of Carlos Arniches, and the sentimental melodramas of the Quintero brothers were frequent sources of screen adaptations.

The eminent playwright Jacinto Benavente founded his own production company, Madrid-Cines, in 1919, the year after another director, José Buchs, had made an unsuccessful movie of Benavente's masterpiece, *Los intereses creados*. His popular *La malquerida* had been filmed in 1914. But Benavente's work as a producer-director was not what he had hoped. Critics lamented that playwrights only made movies after their theater careers were over.[4] In 1934 Benavente joined fellow dramatists, the Quintero brothers, Muñoz Seca, and Eduardo Marquina in forming one of the most important production studios in Spain, CEA (Cinematografía Española-Americana).

The arrival of *cine sonoro* (sound movies) marks a turning point in Spain as elsewhere. Many thought it was only a passing fad, among them Benavente, who claimed sound was only *un ensayo,* a fleeting experiment.[5] Stage and screen stars who could sing, such as Imperio Argentina and Estrellita Castro, welcomed sound. Others, including Margarita Xirgu, dropped their movie careers. La Xirgu, however, did appear in a 1938 screen version of García Lorca's *Bodas de sangre* (*Blood Wedding*) in

Argentina, where she had emigrated before the outbreak of the Civil War.

Indigenous and original talent had arisen in Spain to meet the technological challenge of motion pictures, yet sound movies found no such enthusiasm. Spain, like the Soviet Union, which sent Eisenstein to Hollywood to study sound techniques, was not ready for sound. Spanish film, however, had developed nothing as imaginative as the Soviet school of documentary and could not resist the onslaught of foreign film. It was in the transition from silent movies to sound during the 1930s that foreign film invaded and began its long occupation of Spanish screens.

Spanish viewers had always preferred silent movies made in their own country. "Entre Greta Garbo con letreros o Antoñita Colmé hablando con acento andaluz, los espectadores escogían sin dudarlo la película de esta última" (Between Greta Garbo in subtitles or Antoñita Colmé speaking with her Andalusian accent, spectators always chose the latter),[6] explains Vizcaíno Casas. Sound, however, changed this. Talkies required dubbing, which was better understood than subtitles by a nation in which illiteracy was still widespread. It was, unfortunately, popular outcry against incompetent dubbing which led to the first calls for censorship, not of content but of Spanish dubbing of foreign-language films.

A deluge of American movies flooded Spanish screens. Especially beloved by the poets and artists of Spain's famous literary Generation of 1927, which included García Lorca, Rafael Alberti, Salvador Dalí, and Luis Buñuel, were the comedies of Chaplin, Keaton, the Marx brothers, and Laurel and Hardy. The Spanish public at large was particularly fond of American musicals such as *Broadway Melody* with Eleanor Powell and *Top Hat* with Fred Astaire and Ginger Rogers. The Hollywood star system literally outshone the home product, so that Spaniards deserted their national cinema in droves. This preference only increased in the post–Civil War years.

American incursion into Spanish cinema, which reached alarming proportions in the 1950s, actually benefited the Spanish industry in the 1930s. An example of this is the establishment in 1932 of a distributor for Columbia Pictures in Valencia. With infusion of Spanish oil capital from tycoon don Manuel Casanova, this distributorship was transformed into CIFESA (Compañía Industrial del Film Español, S.A.), Spain's longest-lived and most powerful film-production company.

CIFESA mirrored the political events of the times. After Franco's victory it became known as the studio which most faithfully collaborated by portraying his regime favorably. During the years of the Second Republic, however, from 1932 to 1935, CIFESA was among the few Spanish studios able to successfully resist the rising tide of foreign films. Pre–Civil War CIFESA films included efforts to portray authentic and lively images of Spanish life and culture. Among the best known of these was the sound version of *La hermana de San Sulpicio* (*The Sister of San Sulpicio*) (1934), directed by Florián Rey and starring his wife, Imperio Argentina. Benito Perojo, one of Spain's best pre–Civil War directors, adapted a screen version of the popular *zarzuela*, or operetta, by Bretón de los Herreros, *La verbena de la paloma* (*The Festival of the Dove*) (1935). *Paloma* is notable not only because it includes the first color segment in Spanish cinema but also because of its elaborate scenes of the 1890s created by scenographer Santiago Ontoñón, who had designed sets for García Lorca's traveling theater La Barraca, included street scenes of the Verbena, or popular fiesta in Madrid, with children dancing to organ-grinder music and interiors of working-class homes, as well as cafés and upper-class salons. The unique harmony between social classes conveyed in *Paloma* was not to be repeated in Spanish cinema.

Other quality films with wide popular appeal from CIFESA included *Nobleza baturra* (1935) and *Morena clara* (1936). They sustained Spain's own star system by featuring Spain's beloved Imperio Argentina. Along with *La reina mora* (1936), starring Raquel Rodrigo, these films earned CIFESA sufficient financial stability so that the studio could maintain a cohesive technical crew and plan a range of films aimed at different segments of the public. Among these projects were documentaries, which attracted the talent of one of Spain's most versatile filmmakers, Carlos Velo.

Born in the Galician capital of Santiago de Compostela, Carlos Velo had, like Buñuel, studied with the eminent Cándido Bolívar, Spanish entomologist and director of the Natural History Museum in Madrid. To complete his doctoral research on bees, Velo made a sixteen-mm film illustrating the ability of the queen bee to control the worker bees of a hive. Velo's interest in documentary grew and in 1935 he and critic Fernando Matilla made for CIFESA a series of films, including *Felipe II y el Escorial, Castillos de castilla*, and *Almadrabas*, based on the lives of Galician tuna fishermen. The following year Velo was awarded his first film prize at the International Exposition in Paris by a jury which included Buñuel, whom Velo did not yet know.

Inspired by Robert Flaherty, Velo was working on a film about Morocco when the Civil War erupted. He fled to France and the Moroccan film was finished by others in Berlin. Some of its best footage was used by Carlos Arévalo in the postwar military paean *Harka* (1940). Like Buñuel, Velo pursued his film career in Mexico. Before his death, he worked with Buñuel on *Nazarín* as production consultant and headed Churrubusco Studios' documentary department.

While Spanish cinema in its first forty years did not achieve anything like the international acclaim it attracted during its second forty years, it was not the complete failure some critics declare. Not only was a sufficiently strong industrial base established for war-time conversion to newsreel and documentary production in 1936, but an indigenous school of documentary also emerged from the work of Carlos Velo that served as a point of departure for the Civil War documentaries. In 1937, the Catalán government in Barcelona set up Laya Films, a studio named after a former producing company of the early 1930s, that produced both newsreels and documentaries for the Republican side. CIFESA assumed equivalent duties for Franco's Nationalists.

Perhaps the most significant accomplishment of pre–Civil War film was the elaboration of a genuine artistic expression of national life and culture, a task that had to be entirely redone after the Civil War. In a nation which entered the twentieth century with two-thirds of its adult population living in rural areas[7] and 63 percent of its work force engaged in agricultural labor,[8] the creation in forty years of an industry based on new technology was a major undertaking. That the fulfillment of its promise was to come in a time of lowest national morale—the post–Civil War years—is a measure of the talent and creativity the new industry attracted.

# 2. Censorship: 1939–1975

*En distintas ocasiones ha sido expuesta la necesidad de una intervención celosa y constante del Estado en orden a la educación política y moral de los españoles.*

(On different occasions the necessity has arisen to exercise a zealous and constant intervention by the State into the political and moral education of Spaniards).                                —Ministerial Order of July 15, 1939[1]

Had it not cost so much in terms of freedom of expression and creativity, the story of Spanish film censorship would be amusing. Among its more comic effects were the shift of the lovers' relationship from unmarried man and woman to brother and sister in *Mogambo*—censors appeared to prefer incest to adultery. Sudden withdrawal from distribution of films already approved and the swelling of the French border town of Perpignan from a population of 100,000 to several hundred thousand inhabitants on weekends when Spanish film buffs came to view films that were censored at home are two more examples of the absurdity of film censorship in Spain. Yet Franco's censors, who set to work in 1937, did not have to look far to find living models of fascist film industry.

The most elaborate film studios in Europe were only next door in Italy. Cinecittá, which churned out fascist propaganda films, opened in 1937. Its financial, bureaucratic, and political operations were closely paralleled in Spain. The Italian bureaucratic structure, set up in 1935, made the Direzione Generale per la Cinematografia part of the Ministerio per la Cultura Populare. This structure was later reflected in Spain when the Dirección General de Teatro y Cine became part of the Ministerio de Información y Turismo. The financial practice of providing rebates to film producers according to their box-office earnings was another idea Spain borrowed from its Italian prototype.

Mussolini refused to allow any foreign-language film into Italy, a measure which Franco also adopted. The Italian documentary and educational film company, L'Unione Cinematográfica Educativa (LUCE), became the only producer of fascist documentaries to make and show newsreels in Italy. Spain, too, controlled newsreels and documentaries so that only the state's version of film news could be seen in cinemas throughout the country.

Fascist control of film in Italy functioned at most for a decade. With the defeat of the Axis in 1945, the reaction of film directors against state control speeded the development of Italian neorealism, one of the richest contributions ever made to the art of cinema. In Spain, however, the only undefeated fascist government in Europe continued to exercise rigorous film censorship for over four decades. After the Civil War, Spanish film never developed spontaneously. In fact, it almost ceased to function except as the state's chief means of legitimizing the Franco regime and defending its ideology.[2] A brief chronological review of each decade's censorship practices reveals intricate manipulation, hypocrisy, often ignorance, and always the persistence of the most sustained effort anywhere in Western Europe to control a national film industry.

The first effort of the Franco regime to censor films began as a wartime measure when in July 1937 censorship offices—the Junta Superior de Censura—were established in Seville and Salamanca. This five-man board of censors grew to a minimum of twenty in 1968 and saw many changes in administrative structure and reorganization. Two measures begun in 1937—prior submission of film scripts and censorship of foreign films entering Spain—became ineradicable mainstays of censorship and were continued in varying degrees throughout the *franquista* period.

Other cornerstones of censorship were laid in the 1940s. Obligatory dubbing, imposed in 1941, made the showing of original versions of foreign films illegal unless they were first dubbed in Spanish studios. Franco's ban of foreign languages even extended to regional languages spoken within his own country, such as Catalán, which was also prohibited in films. In December 1942 another blow to free expression was delivered with the formation of No-Do, the state monopoly of news and documentary film. Perhaps the most devastating device applied to Spanish film was the granting of import and dubbing licenses to Spanish producers. According to the "quality" of each film they produced, censors (the Comisión Clasificadora) granted Spanish producers permits to import foreign films. Needless to say, prior censorship of Spanish filmscripts made Spanish films less competitive with foreign ones. With the added incentive of larger profits made by importing the more marketable foreign product, Spanish producers could now safely ignore the quality of Spanish films. Thus, the practice, rewarded by the state, of making a conventional vehicle for fascist mythology in order to be able to import more foreign films became entrenched. Spanish viewers naturally preferred the less censored product, demoralizing efforts of Spanish directors to treat national problems in their films.

To counter the public preference for the less censored foreign films, a designation of "Películas de interés nacional" (films of national interest) was created in 1944. This gave recognition and distribution privileges to films "cuyos cuadros artístico y técnico sean esencialmente españoles . . . que la película contenga muestras inequívocas de exaltación de valores raciales o enseñanzas de nuestros principios morales y políticos (whose artistic and technical quality are essentially Spanish . . . the film must contain unequivocal examples advancing racial values or teachings of our moral and political principles").[3] Clearly, fascist films preferred by the Franco regime competed so poorly with foreign products that the state, by this preferential device, had to reward them for their rigor in reflecting fascist values.

On December 13, 1946, the Franco government received a slap from the United Nations in the form of a recommendation that the members of this international body withdraw their embassies from Europe's remaining fascist state. This attempt to isolate Franco may have affected Spanish minds, for the following year, on July 6, 1947, by national referendum, Spain declared itself a monarchy. It established a law of succession that dispelled any dynastic hopes Franco may have had and posed him as regent to be succeeded by a king from Spain's royal house. However remote these events seem from Spanish film, they may have helped the first decade of *franquista* censorship to close with two hopeful events. In February 1947, the first national film school of advanced study, the Instituto de Investigaciones y Experiencias Cinematográficas (IIEC), was created and opened to 109 students. In addition, on December 31, 1947, dubbing of foreign films was ruled no longer obligatory. While the existence of a film school and the opportunity to see original versions of films from other countries seem to suggest progress, the effects of these measures were very slow to take root. Dubbing, now a small industry within Spanish cinema, had become expected by the Spanish public. Almost twenty years passed before original versions were shown to more than a tiny film-club public. Some important foreign films were banned altogether from entering Spain during the decade 1937–1947, including Chaplin's *The Great Dictator* (1940), Jean Renoir's *Rules of the Game* (1939), Luchino Visconti's *Ossessione* (1942) and *La terra trema* (1947), and Rossellini's *Roma, città aperta* (1945) and *Paisá* (1946).

During its first decade Spanish censorship established its practices to the extent that all new developments in cinema, such as Italian neorealism were sealed out. Franco's censors seemed to want to return to the eighteenth century when books by French philosophers and deists such as Voltaire and Montesquieu were banned in hopes that the virus of free thinking might be kept out of Spain.

The early and mid 1950s were years in which the institution of censorship tirelessly met repeated challenges to its absolute authority over the Spanish film industry. In 1951 José María García Escudero, a colonel in the air force's legal department who had written about the question of censorship, was appointed head of the Dirección General de Cinematografía y Teatro. A political moderate, García Escudero defended a controversial film, *Surcos* (1951), in which prostitutes appear. This film, to be discussed in the next chapter, dealt with the very real national problem of the urban migration of the rural poor. That García Escudero occupied his position only six months, to be replaced in February 1952, suggests that the state would not tolerate even occasional portrayal of national problems by filmmakers.

Yet, rewarding filmmakers who made ideological vehicles for the state did not work either. It in fact subsidized an epidemic of undercover trade of import licenses. So a sliding scale of classifications was set up to reward and punish independent films. The first category, "interés nacional," provided a state rebate of 50 percent of production costs; 1A, 40 percent; 1B, 35 percent; 2A, 30 percent; 2B, 25 percent. There was a third class, a kind of cinema Siberia, in which not only did a film receive no state funds, but it also could not be premiered in either of the country's two principal cities. These so-called protection categories were established in 1952, the year Carlos Saura entered the IIEC. In 1959 his *Los golfos,* to be discussed in a later chapter, was one of the victims of a 2B classification. Berlanga's *Bienvenido, Mr. Marshall* was also made in 1952. It was not among the chosen films "de interés nacional." Although it dealt honestly with national problems, outmoded vehicles such as *Catalina de Inglaterra, Alba de America,* and *Sor Intrépida* were chosen that year as being more worthy of national interest.

One independent voice was able to make itself heard in 1953 when the film review *Objetivo* began publication. Since 1941 the only national discussion of films took place in the pages of *Primer Plano,* a weekly that was fond of noting Hitler's film preferences and that generally echoed state views on both domestic and international cinema. In its first year *Primer Plano* included articles about the activities of a Falangist film club whose program was carefully designed by the former Spanish dictator José Antonio Primo de Rivera, to "no darle un carácter político. Fue proyectado un inefable *Don Juan Tenorio* y se dio a conocer una película nazi, *Mongerot*" (not give it a political character. A delightful *Don Juan* was shown and the Nazi film *Mongerot* was introduced).[4]

Film magazines were the only means Spaniards had to inform themselves of new developments in foreign film. Since they were generally unable to view innumerable censored films, they were able to learn of the existence, for example, of the school of Soviet documentary only from film magazines. The ideas and issues of neorealism were introduced through *Objetivo.* Although short-lived (dead after nine issues in 1956), experiments such as *Objetivo* were reassuring signs that somewhere in small urban circles there was a public eager for news of film art. *Objetivo* was replaced by *Film Ideal,* a generally conformist yet not stridently fascist journal such as *Primer Plano.*

The year of *Objetivo's* demise was also the year in which Juan Antonio

Bardem, already a major director of independent mind, was arrested while filming *Calle mayor*. The producer tried to replace him, but the star, Betsy Blair, refused to work without Bardem. Because of his role at the Salamanca Talks in 1955, in which he denounced the Spanish film industry, Bardem was watched closely by the state. His *Muerte de un ciclista* (1955) portrayed Spanish society as corrupt and complacent. The wounding of a Falangist student at a political rally in Madrid in 1956 had increased tensions throughout the country so that a general state of crisis prevailed. Several important figures were jailed temporarily, among them Juan Antonio Bardem, who was arrested at his hotel early in the morning of February 12 and released two weeks later with no charges ever being filed against him.

The regime maintained silence regarding Bardem's detention. It was not reported by British journalists but leaked to France because *Calle mayor* was a co-production with a French film producer. Protest was registered loudly by prestigious French intellectuals, including Jean-Paul Sartre and Jean Cocteau. By the time a Spanish negotiating team in Paris prepared to renew a trade agreement pertaining to film industry coproductions, Bardem had been released without official explanation or comment. So, while film censorship usually took the form of cutting scripts and scenes from footage already shot, on rare occasions it simply imprisoned a film director.

Spaniards were still "protected" from reality as it was being portrayed in foreign films. While *Gone with the Wind* (1939) was finally released in Spain in 1950, Zavattini's *Amore in Città* (1953) was banned. This was also the year of the retouching of *Mogambo* and the elimination of the beach scene from Academy Award–winner *From Here to Eternity* (1953). Scenes referring to the Spanish Civil War were cut from *Snows of Kilimanjaro* (1952) because they portrayed the Republican (losing) side. As Spain began its third decade of censorship, two incidents resulting from the focus of international attention upon Spanish censorship helped subvert its efforts. In 1959, Carlos Saura made *Los golfos,* an uncompromising look at urban youth unemployment. It was banned four times before it was finally condemned by a 2B rating.

Though *Los golfos* was delayed opening in Madrid for two years, it was shown at the Cannes Film Festival and thus gained international recognition. This unexpected boost was possible because in 1960 a new official committee was selected to choose the films that would represent Spain at international festivals. While Falangist José Luis Sáenz de Heredia headed this commission, it also included Juan Antonio Bardem and other film professionals who represented the industry and not the administration, as did the censors.

The other event that helped focus international ridicule upon Spanish censorship was the success of Buñuel's *Viridiana* at Cannes where, in 1961, it won the Palma de Oro, or first prize. This award was the first ever for Spain and was accepted by the director general of the Departmento de Cinematografía y Teatro, José Muñoz Fontán. Among Spain's most famous emigrés, Buñuel had been invited to film in Spain with Uninci, a Spanish production company headed by Juan Antonio Bardem. Buñuel submitted the script of *Viridiana* to the censors, who requested only one change. In the final scene Viridiana, instead of entering Jorge's bed, joins him and his maid at a table where the three begin a card game. Buñuel declared this change strengthened the film by making its conclusion less obvious.

When *Viridiana* won acclaim at Cannes, however, it was assailed by the conservative Catholic *L'Osservatore Romano*. Perhaps more sensitive to cinema because their national film industry was among the most advanced, Italian Catholics were horrified to see the Last Supper parodied in a freeze shot of inebriated beggars and other unusual jokes about Catholic dogma. The final scene suggested to them a ménage à trois between the three central characters. An embarrassed Spanish government found it necessary to prohibit the showing of its only first prize–winning film. Mention of it was prohibited in the Spanish press. Muñoz Fontán was immediately replaced by the Falangist Jesús Suevos, Uninci was dissolved, and a new dark age threatened the Spanish film industry.

*Viridiana* was not seen in Spain for sixteen years. Only due to the foresight of Buñuel himself, who took a copy of the film with him from Madrid to Paris, was the world able to see this remarkable work. Such incidents helped explain the lament of Spanish film critics such as Francisco Pérez Dolz Riba who wondered, "¿Quiere España tener un cine propio? Yo creo que no" (Does Spain want to have its own cinema? I think not).[5]

Only economic necessity was able to force cultural change in Spain. In 1962, when Spain first tried to join the European Common Market, fresh faces were added to the government. Among them was García Escudero, the moderate dismissed ten years before, who was now restored as director of Cinematografía y Teatro. García Escudero's direction of Spanish censorship is generally described as neither conservative nor liberal but as *aperturista*, of relative openness toward Western attitudes and customs.

García Escudero was able to institute the first substantive change in Spanish censorship when, in 1963, he insisted that the criteria of censorship be spelled out. After ten years of repeated requests by filmmakers, a specific list of prohibited topics was published. Among banned subjects were those favoring divorce, abortion, euthanasia, and birth control and those appearing to justify adultery, prostitution, and illicit sexual behavior. In spite of its length of censored topics, publication of this list constituted an advance. No longer could a film be prohibited for simply offending military, religious, or political groups, thanks to the clearly stated "Normas Cinematográficas" of 1963.

One result of *apertura*, a moment of censorship's lowered profile, is the case of Belanga's *El verdugo* (*The Executioner*), which was approved after cuts totalling 4.3 minutes were made. This film, discussed in detail in Chapter 4, is a comic treatment of the position of public executioner, a role which many saw as an open satire of Franco.

Entirely by coincidence, three political executions were carried out in 1963, the year *El verdugo* was made. Communist Julián Grimau was executed in April for unspecified activities committed during the Civil War.[6] Two anarchists—Francisco Granados Gata and Joaquín Delgado Martínez—became political victims of the state and were executed in August. These highly visible punishments made Berlanga's film seem intended as protest and ridicule of the chief of state. The Spanish ambassador to Italy, Alfredo Sánchez Bella, vigorously objected to *El verdugo* and tried to have it banned. When he was informed that such efforts were too late, the ambassador brought attention to the film as an example of the tolerance of Spanish censorship.

Six years later, however, Sánchez Bella's opportunity to influence Spanish film arrived when he was appointed to succeed the ousted García Escudero. Sánchez Bella promptly closed the crack in the façade of Spanish censorship by banning Fellini's *Satyricon* (1969) and *Roma* (1972) and by rescinding permission to show the great Italian director's landmark *La dolce vita* (1959), still unseen in Spain. A documentary of the years 1940 to 1970 compiled by young Spanish director Basilio Martín Patino, already viewed five times and approved by censors, was also banned by Sánchez Bella. His administration cut Saura's *El jardín de las delicias* (1970), then delayed its release for six months.

These reversals, accompanied by the government's failure to pay legally established subsidies, brought the Spanish film industry to a state of crisis. Faulty from the outset, this protection system gave preference to films that were faithful to the moral precepts of the dictatorship. The assignment of categories became so arbitrary that it was easier for a producer to inflate the budget of a film that had already won a favorable rating rather than hope others of his films would reap equally favorable ratings. Thus quality became synonymous with expensive extravaganzas which exalted heroic and patriotic deeds, religious devotion, and other concepts of the fascist mythology.

The failure of government subsidies drastically reduced the viability of an industry which had never been fully independent economically of the state. Economic dependency, in itself a measure of censorship, together with restrictive moral and social attitudes and increasing competition from television threatened to make the decade of the 1970s among the

Spanish film industry's worst since the Civil War. The state's action in this crisis was typified in its prohibition of public discussion of the industry's problems planned by the Madrid Club Corral de Comedias in February 1970.

The following two years—1973 and 1974—were marked by considerable political unrest in Spain. Franco appointed his close personal friend and staunch ally, Luis Carrero Blanco, president on the premise that he would introduce no radical changes in the government. On December 20, 1973, Carrero Blanco was assassinated. He was replaced by Carlos Arias Navarro, who handed the Ministry of Information and Tourism to Pío Cabanillas.

It was during Cabanillas's administration that the first full-shot female nude appeared in a Spanish film. María José Cantudo is reflected nude very briefly in a mirror in *La trastienda* (1974), a film discussed as much for its portrayal of its lead male role as for the less-than-thirty-seconds of a female nude. Cabanillas became known as *aperturista,* or a moderate, not only because of *La trastienda* but also because of the *succès de scandale* of Saura's *La prima Angélica* (1974).

The script of *La prima Angélica* was first rejected by censors in October 1973. After a second rejection it was finally approved and shown to five ministers of the government. All five opposed its release. By the time they screened it, however, *La prima Angélica* had been sent to Cannes, where it won a special jury prize for best director. On May 13, 1974, eight right-wing youths broke into the projection booth of the Cine Amaya in Palma de Mallorca and stole several reels of *La prima Angélica*. In July, the Cine Balmés in Barcelona incurred damage from a fire bomb during a showing of the film. On October 29, Franco removed Cabanillas from his post as minister. When the Cine Balmés reopened, it eliminated the film from its programming.

Public outcry both in favor of and against *La prima Angélica* opened a national dialogue on the long-silent topic of the Civil War. Newspapers throughout the country received letters and published cartoons and articles on the merits of the film and the risk it posed to national dignity. "Lo cierto es," concluded critic Diego Galán, "que *Prima Angélica* ha pasado al baúl de los recuerdos familiares" (The truth is that *Prima Angélica* has indeed gotten to the bottom of our trunk of national memories).[7] The turbulent reception of this film reveals a Spanish public still unable, in 1974, to accept peaceably the memories of those who lost the Civil War.

Nine months before Franco's death three changes appeared in the revised censorship code in February 1975. The negative language of the 1963 code is revised into a less direct, more positive statement: "Se prohibirá" (it shall be forbidden) becomes "se considerará contraria a una recta conciencia colectiva siempre que se traten de justificarse . . . la presentación de" (the presentation of . . . will be considered contrary to a suitable collective conscience).[8] The list of prohibited topics is the same as that of 1963 with the exception of divorce, which is not mentioned. Finally, article nine of the revision allows "el desnudo, siempre que esté exigido por la unidad total del film" (the nude, as long as it is required by the total unity of the film). The revised code concluded by rejecting all pornographic images of nudes.

After Franco's death in November 1975, censorship withered considerably but did not entirely disappear. The requirement for prior censorship of scripts was abolished for Spanish films, but still required of foreign films shot in Spain. Most of the more rigid prohibitions of specific themes and of eroticism were lifted in 1976, although some themes, such as a satire of the military, remain difficult to deal with even today. The only official censorship remaining is a board of classification which assigns a rating to each film according to its public "suitability."

Part of the story of censorship lies in the results it produced and in the devices designed by film-industry professionals to subvert it. Thirty-six years of rigid limitations left the industry both culturally and economically disadvantaged, yet directors, actors, and producers somehow managed to continue working. A brief review of some of the results of censorship can illustrate some of the dimensions of three decades of enforced compliance to the moral codes of a fascist dictatorship.

One of the few ways a heavily censored Spanish director could reach an international public was to participate in coproductions (copros). Foreign film companies, with more money to spend on movies than was available in Spain, found filming there a bargain. Competent Spanish actors and technicians were eager to work at minimal salaries. The Franco government saw a chance for one of its sickest industries to continue functioning with an infusion of funds from other countries. So the system appeared to please everyone. The copro bonanza reached its height in the mid 1950s. In 1956, for example, seventy-six films were made in Spain, twenty-two (almost one-third) of which were copros.

The system, however, soon broke down. While foreign funds put Spanish film professionals to work, they also raised production costs to levels entirely out of reach of Spanish directors. Actors who had been paid enormous salaries for small parts in Italian and American films were no longer interested in working in low-paying Spanish productions. Most of the lead roles in copros were reserved for famous stars, while Spanish actors and actresses were left with minimal roles.

American companies devised what the Spanish view as reverse colonization in which the copro exploited Spain beyond any possible mutual benefit. Beginning in 1955 with Robert Rossen's *Alexander the Great,*

American super productions were made in Spain with little concern for quality or cooperation. Samuel Bronston's *John Paul Jones* (1959) included only token participation by Suevia Films, while Nicolas Ray's *King of Kings* actually incurred financial losses to Spanish industry. When Samuel Bronston acquired the Spanish studio Estudios Chamartín, the Franco government began to suspect that copros were no longer the benefit they once seemed. Economic loss was compounded by cultural humiliation when *El Cid* (1960), based on Spain's national epic poem, turned into what Marta Hernández terms "a medieval western," starring Charlton Heston and Sophia Loren.[9] In April 1964, the government passed a regulation requiring copros to maintain a level of "aesthetic quality and be approved by the Ministry of Commerce."[10]

When the copros encountered Spanish censorship, another abuse arose which underscored the obsolescence of Spanish films. The practice of rushing two versions of a copro—one for Spain and one for the rest of the world—began in 1954 when the firm of José Luis Sáenz de Heredia, director of the famous *Raza* (1941), began the production of *The Princess at Eboli* with a British company. The script was rejected by Spanish censors, so two versions of the picture were shot and distributed. Naturally, Spaniards saw only the censored version. The uncut version was distributed in Britain and elsewhere. The practice of double versions shamefully patronized the Spanish public. It also was a hypocritical acknowledgment by censors that their work, outside the protection of the fascist state, could not stand on its own in the modern world.

While production of two versions of a film blatantly discriminated against Spanish viewers, censors actually caused two versions of foreign films to exist by distributing cut versions of them in Spain or by changing their meaning so as to radically alter their character. The best known example of this is the work of Ingmar Bergman, whose films were distorted so as to make this disturbing director appear to be an orthodox Catholic to an uninformed Spanish public. The rape scene from *The Virgin Spring* (1956) was cut, as were scenes showing women in roles other than satisfied wives and mothers. Scenes of the tormented women of *Persona* (1967) and *Cries and Whispers* (1973) were accompanied by explanatory subtitles or dialogue was dubbed. Others such as *Silence* (1963) and *Hour of the Wolf* (1968) were banned. So, in fact, there existed two versions of Ingmar Bergman—the original and the one for Spain.

Bergman is a director whose work Spanish censors could modify to suit their needs. Federico Fellini, on the other hand, was hopelessly out of the censor's reach. Nothing could touch Fellini's visual parodies and outrageous scenes, so his films were not tampered with but simply banned. Fellini's films are often hilarious fantasies in which reality serves only as a point of departure. In Spain, both fantasy and reality were banned through prohibition of both documentary shorts and newsreels. No-Do (*noticias documentales*) was the only official view of daily reality allowed on Spanish screens. Thus, as another effect of censorship, an entire genre, that of documentary, withered in Spain. The existence of a Soviet school of documentary was now only rumor, since these films had not been seen in Spain since before the Civil War.

Banned since its debut at a small private screening in Madrid in 1932 was Buñuel's documentary on Las Hurdes, a poor mountainous region which has been called Spain's Appalachia. *Las Hurdes (Tierra sin pan)* was acclaimed abroad as "probably one of the most outstanding films of the thirties"[11] and could have served as the basis for the development of documentary film in Spain. But by imposing No-Do as the only view of reality available to Spaniards, censorship successfully blocked experimentation in the fields of film essay, newsreels, and documentary.

The refusal to allow documentary filmmaking was a logical result of Franco's attitude toward documentary footage of the Civil War, which apparently is still sealed from public view. Documentaries made by foreigners, such as André Malraux's *Espoir* (1937) and Frédéric Rossif's *Mourir en Madrid* (1963), were also banned as was the treatment of the Civil War from the Republican perspective. Even as a theme in fictional films, the Civil War was forbidden to be viewed by Spaniards except from a victor's standpoint. *For Whom the Bell Tolls* (1943) was prohibited in Spain, while scenes of the Spanish conflict were cut from *The Snows of Kilimanjaro* (1952).

To a curious public wondering about the footage of the Civil War, the Falangist film journal *Primer Plano* directed a brief, unsigned article affirming, "También la cámara de cine estuvo en la guerra" (the movie camera was also in the war). The article was accompanied by a picture of General Franco with a camera crew. The article informs us that "en la lucha nació el Departamento Nacional de Cinematografía por feliz iniciativa del Caudillo" (the National Department of Film was born in the Civil War, thanks to our leaders).[12] This kind of coverage set the tone for the No-Do newsreels, whose documentary of national life remained at this uninformative level until El Caudillo's death in 1975.

Censorship was the central fact of cultural life in Spain for thirty-eight years. Because of it, most Spanish artists, writers, and intellectuals were forced to live and work abroad to fully develop their thought. The list of Spanish émigrés is long and includes some of our century's most gifted minds—Picasso, Buñuel, Pablo Casals. Like art and literature in Franco's Spain, film under censorship did not disappear but developed distortions characterizing it as art produced under one of Europe's most enduring dictatorships of our century.

# 3. Early Postwar Film: 1939–1959

Franco's triumph over the badly split labor-liberal-socialist factions which made up the Republican side in the Civil War was absolute. He demanded and won unconditional surrender. This demand for absolute authority characterized the postwar period. Leftist leaders not killed during the Civil War were shot soon after.[1] Supporters of the former Republican government were left destitute in a mass redistribution of jobs. Opposition was not tolerated by Franco's repressive regime, which took merciless reprisal against the losers. The regime not only heavily censored works of artists and intellectuals who remained in the country but used the mass media to legitimate its actions.

The major genres of Spanish film during the first two postwar decades include the *cine cruzada,* or Civil War films, historical extravaganzas, *cine de sacerdotes,* or religious films, and the folklore musicals. All these film genres presented Spain as it was in the past. They upheld and reinforced the traditional views of church and fascist state to which Franco's victory gave the force of law. These genres all had a common goal of reassuring Spaniards that, notwithstanding the devastating Civil War, their country's values and institutions had not changed. Perhaps the most important, and most carefully crafted by censorship, were the war films which, after all, were the only images most Spaniards had of their country's recent history.

War films exhorting the values and triumph of Franco's forces served not only to justify the Civil War but also to extend sympathy for the fascist victory into the postwar peace. The prototype of the Spanish Civil War epic was, not surprisingly, directed by an Italian, Augusto Genina, who had wide experience in the glorification of fascism under Mussolini. Known in Spain as *Sin novedad en el alcázar* (*Siege of the Alcázar*), Genina's film was shot in Spain in 1940. It exalts the patriotism and sacrifice of the Nationalist general Moscardó whose refusal to yield to the Republican siege of the military academy at Toledo led to the death of his son Luis, held hostage by the Republicans. Genina conceived of *Alcázar* in

Alfredo Mayo as young General Franco in *Raza* (1941).

grandiose terms as "the *Potemkin* of the constructive revolution."[2] With swelling, almost operatic music, the film evokes both exuberance and terror. Its final scene of triumphant Nationalists saluting with outstretched arms creates an image of the Civil War as a twentieth-century crusade against evil infidels.

Franco himself, however, set the example for Civil War films by writing a book, *Raza,* then hiring José Luis Sáenz de Heredia, nephew of former dictator Primo de Rivera, to produce a script and direct a movie based on it. *Raza,* written under the pseudonym of Jaime de Andrade, focuses with considerable biographical detail upon a fictional military family whose son becomes a hero in the Spanish Civil War. The conflict is referred to as *la cruzada* (the crusade) with no attempt to hide disgust for the Republicans, identified with the code words "puppets of Freemasonry."

This incredible fictionalized self-portrait narrates the military exploits of its hero, José Churruca, like Franco an infantryman. Again like Franco, José is shot but miraculously recovers. Following the events of the Caudillo's life, José goes to Madrid to meet his sweetheart and to participate in the victory march through the streets. The film was advertised as *cine patriótico* and was dedicated to "las juventudes de España . . . Que así es España y así es la raza" (Spanish youth . . . since this is how Spain is and this is what the Cause is like).[3] That *Primer Plano,* the state's movie magazine, chose to apply Genina's phrase to *Raza* and advertise it as "el Potemkin del franquismo"[4] is ironic, both in its indirect praise of Eisenstein's masterpiece and in the apparent assumption that the phrase would be understood. Since Eisenstein's films had all been prohibited in Spain, few Spanish viewers could have known what *Potemkin* was.

During the three decades following the Civil War, only forty-five films dealt with the topic of the conflict and only twenty-one of these showed combat scenes. The rest made allusion to the Civil War to dramatize other themes.[5] Among those twenty-one were two about the heroics of Franco's aviators, *Escuadrilla (Squadron)* (1941) and *Héroes del aire (Air Heroes)* (1957). In the former, the role of Carlos de Haya, Franco's personal pilot, is prominent, while the latter is a variation on the theme of pilots' bravery. The navy received its accolades in *Servicio al mar* (1950), which recounts the submarine blockade of Republican ships. The infantry had to wait until 1959, when Pedro Lazaga portrayed its gallantry in *La fiel infantería (The Faithful Infantry)*.

A popular variation on the theme of military bravery was *Harka* (1940), directed by Carlos Arévalo. Its Arabic title is the name of a military garrison in Morocco where Spain occupied its last colonial territory. Since scenes of Moors attacking Spaniards were banned, skirmishes take place against an unseen enemy. The narrative centers upon the sense of duty of Luis, played by Luis Peña, a young lieutenant who falls in love with Amparo. This female lead is played by the talented Luchy Soto who, thirty years later, plays some memorable roles in Carlos Saura's films. Amparo insists that Luis leave the military and marry her, but in Madrid Luis becomes nostalgic for his battalion. He returns to Morocco and, over a drink in the officers' club, confesses his dilemma to his captain, a fiercely patriotic career officer. "Don't you ever need tenderness?" Luis inquires, as the arch-hero of Spanish fascist film, Alfredo Mayo, responds with an angry glare. His tight facial muscles constrict in a grimace of discipline. Standing suddenly, the captain approaches a dancing couple, pushes the young woman's partner aside, and begins dancing with her. Luis and the irritated dancing partner stare in wonder at the captain's rude fury which, in the absence of any explanation, can only be interpreted to mean that upon the rare occasion when the captain needs tenderness, he takes what he finds.

Luis follows his captain's example and chooses his battalion over marriage. As the film ends he addresses new recruits at the garrison with the same words his colonel had used when he first arrived as a young officer. Without obvious enemies or the well-defined fascist cause which motivates soldiers in the Civil War films, *Harka* nevertheless carries on the worn fascist myth of posing women and marriage as primary obstacles to the fulfillment of military duty.

*Harka* repeats the rhetoric of militarism for its own sake, a natural out-growth of two decades of war films glorifying Franco's triumph. Roland Barthes reminds us in his essay "Le Mythe aujourd'hui" that one major way myth retains its power is by frequent recurrence. The mythology of military patriotism was kept alive by re-releasing *Raza* in 1950. With a new sound track and revised dialogue, it was retitled *El espíritu de la raza* (*Spirit of the Cause*) and covered three decades of Spanish military his-tory: the 1898 loss of Spain's American colonies, fragmentation of Span-ish political factions of 1928, and, the longest part of the film, the Civil War of 1936–1939. Each segment reminds viewers of the sacrifice of mili-tary service and the honor of dying for the defense of the nation.

Use of religious rhetoric and vocabulary to describe the Civil War was a natural extension of Franco's designation of the conflict as a "crusade" in *Raza*. In Spain, where church and state have never been entirely separate, it was almost inevitable that films with religious themes constitute one of the major genres of post–Civil War cinema. Some repeated the motif of the holy war, such as *El santuario no se rinde* (*The Sanctuary Will Not Surrender*) (1948), which dramatizes the defense of the Sanctuary of the Virgin de la Cabeza. In others, the central character of a soldier priest continued the action of the war films dressed in cassock instead of uni-form. Among these are *Cerca del cielo* (*Close to Heaven*) (1951), which deals with the bishop of Teruel, Father Polanco, who fell victim to the Civil War, and *El frente infinito* (*The Infinite Front Line*) (1956), which glorifies the life of a chaplain. One of the most popular films of 1950 was Nieves Conde's *Balarrasa*. Influenced by the American *Keys to the King-dom*, *Balarrasa* narrates the temptations of a young priest, except that Balarrasa, the Spanish priest, is only faintly tempted by evil.

In religious films under Franco, all priests were admirable individuals willing to give their lives, if necessary, to defend the moral values es-poused by the loyal Catholic Franco regime. Leftist or populist priests, many of whom supported the Nationalist side during the Civil War, sim-ply were not portrayed on screen. Nuns, however, were popular subjects of Spanish postwar films. The best-known of these was *La hermana San Sulpicio*, based on Armando Palacio Valdéz's nineteenth-century novel of Andalusian manners. It was made into its second film version in 1952 by Luis Lucia. Carmen Sevilla, one of Spain's leading folkloric actresses, plays the role of Gloria, the young Andalusian woman who, as a result of a misunderstanding with her mother, is sent to a convent at the age of nineteen.

The self-serving rhetoric of the *franquista* war films diminished as the decades passed and the Civil War receded in the public mind. It does not disappear but is merely draped in period costume in historical extrava-ganzas so numerous that they form a genre by themselves. Of course,

Franco did not invent the use of history as screen propaganda. Again, Italy provides a model. The faithful fascist director Alessandro Blasetti justified historical analogy for political purposes, explaining, "A historical film can evoke moments perfectly analogical with those we live in. Those moments and references can serve as a learning experience for the people of today."[6] The historical war epics differ from their modern counterparts primarily in their period settings, for their ideological basis is the same. Imperial attitudes of sacrifice, patriotism, and military glory coincide neatly with the values of Franco's fascism. In them, individual heroism and nationalism predominate, while social history or collective action is almost entirely lacking.

Hero/heroine worship within the context of imperial exploits generated a series of films about Spanish queens, including *Inés de Castro* (1944), which recalls a fourteenth-century civil war; *Reina santa* (1946), recounting the life of Queen Isabella; and *Locura de amor* (1948), narrating the life of Ferdinand and Isabella's daughter, the mad queen Juana, hopelessly in love with her consort, Philip of Burgundy. *Locura de amor,* starring the young Aurora Bautista, was one of the biggest hits of the period and made millions for CIFESA, the film company that churned out most of the regime's historical and war epics. As in Hollywood, one success called forth almost endless variations on the original theme, so *La leona de Castilla* (1951), *Catalina de Inglaterra* (1951), *Doña María la Brava* (1947), and *Augustina de Aragón* (1950) also appeared. The adulation of historical figures easily combined with religious themes to produce a kind of hybrid genre, the historical-religious extravaganza, such as the portrayal of Ignatius de Loyola in *El capitán de Loyola* (1948). Spaniards watched these films because, as the film critic Luciano G. Egido explains, they wanted to believe that, as the dedication of *Raza* put it, "La historia es así" (That's history).[7]

The middle class might have been lulled by war films glorifying Franco's triumph and traditionalists seemed content with images of royal cloaks and swords upon the screen. For the lower classes and the undereducated there was an endless series of folklore films. Most of these, starring flamenco singers such as Carmen Sevilla or Lola Flores, were little more than operettas based on the overworked but ever popular *zarzuelas,* or musical comedies. Among these is *La Dolores* (1940), directed by the competent Florián Rey and starring Conchita Piquer and Manuel Luna.

The opening shot of Dolores milking a cow in a barnyard surrounded by merry, costumed peasants conveyed to Spanish workers that rural life was pleasant. When Dolores lands a job in Calatayud as a barmaid by charming the owners and customers, the message was that staying in your place and putting forth a sunny temperament would land you a job. Dolores, like most of the other women in this film, is a servant who waits on old toothless men dressed in knickers, black jackets, and bandanas seated at tables talking or leaning on their canes. The uneducated but witty Dolores falls for the educated but not very responsible nephew of the owners of the bar. After scenes of the village bullfight, plowing the fields, and the fiesta, the nephew departs, leaving an unsophisticated public reassured that Spain was insulated from change and that unemployment, housing and food shortages, and other problems did not exist.

The southern variant of the folklore genre, the *andaluzada*, underwent slight modernization in *Torbellino* (*Whirlwind*) (1941). Its heroine, played by the pert Estrellita Castro, lured faithful crowds with her Andalusian accent and clear soprano voice. Overcoming innumerable obstacles, she finally connives to audition for the impresario of a radio show in Madrid. Her voice and rendition of songs are irresistible. Soon she returns, triumphant, to Sevilla. Here shots of sunny plazas, cathedrals, and flower-laden balconies remind viewers that Spain is picturesque, a happy place where one can escape the pace of modern life.

Having derived from authentic folklore, the Spanish folklore song and dance films never paralleled the Hollywood musical. Spain's indigenous popular music included the flamenco rhythms and dances, whose most skilled practitioners were stars of the traditional operettas, or *zarzuelas*. Another form of musical was that of child stars Joselito, known as the "golden nightingale," and Marisol. Titles of the films of Joselito, including *El Pequeño ruiseñor* (*The Little Nightingale*) (1956) and *Bello recuerdo* (*Beautiful Memory*) (1961), and of Marisol—*Ha llegado un ángel* (*An Angel Has Arrived*) (1961), *Marisol rumbo a Río* (*Marisol Goes to Río*) (1963), and *Las cuatro bodas de Marisol* (*Marisol's Four Weddings*) (1967)—are testaments that the child-star musical in Spain, like the Shirley Temple films in Hollywood, reached new heights of sentimentalism.

The Spanish film industry's most successful musical, however, is neither folkloric nor sung by a child prodigy. Like these two forms of musicals, *El último cuplé* (*The Last Couplet*) was a melodrama much like *Torbellino*, yet it achieved its goal beyond the fondest dreams of its director, Juan de Orduña, or its star, Sarita Montiel. With *El último cuplé*, the cult of nostalgia reached its apex. It is another sentimental story, this time of a music hall singer, María Luján. María secures success by marrying an empresario but remains unhappy. *El último cuplé* had a first run in Madrid which lasted almost a year. It offered the passions and gallantry of the past, a pistol duel between the impresario and a Russian duke, María's love for a young matador, no on-screen physical intimacy, and a final death scene in which Maria collapses onstage. The evasion of reality won the same adoring public in Latin America as it had in Spain and remains among the greatest commercial successes of 1957, the year of its release, or of any year in the history of Spanish film.

The predominant film genres of the 1940s and 1950s—those of military triumph, both historical and current, of religious heroism, of escapist folklore and melodrama—reflect a film industry manipulated by the state in order to pacify the two conflicting economic classes of the postwar era. Exceptions to these genres were few and unsuccessful. Expression of eroticism in film was prohibited during the 1940s and 1950s. During these two decades it also remained impossible to deal with social problems in Spanish film. The fact that an attempt, however feeble, was made to create authentic, realistic films is a tribute to the persistence and imagination of those who dared to risk their careers and deal with current topics. Among them was José Antonio Nieves Conde, a loyal Franco supporter. His *Surcos* (*Furrows*) (1951) was based on a script by the novelist Gonzálo Torrente Ballester, once a film censor, and Natividad Zoro.

*Surcos* narrates the story of rural immigration to the city, a problem that has plagued Spain for two centuries and is central in Luis Martín Santos's masterpiece of postwar fiction, *Tiempo de silencio* (*Time of Silence*) (1961). Scenes considered offensive in *Surcos* included those of city slums crowded with prostitutes and swindlers, filthy rooms, and a woman smoking a cigarette on an unmade bed. Intolerable, too, were concluding frames in which a young girl accompanying her family on their return to their village from the unholy city decides to jump off the train. This apparent choice of urban deprivation over starvation in the village caused a scandal.

García Escudero, director of the government's Departamento de Cinematografía y Teatro, defended *Surcos* on the grounds that it carried no economic or political thesis, but the ending of *Surcos* was censored and, in February 1952, García Escudero was replaced. Nieves Conde recalled that *Surcos* was "una pequeña isla en el cine español y en mi carrera" (a little island in Spanish film and in my career), one way of saying that this unique film did not conform to the triumphal, escapist genres of postwar Spanish film.[8]

Undaunted and apparently galvanized by his brush with censorship, Nieves Conde continued working in a critical vein with *Los peces rojos* (*The Red Fish*) (1955), *Todos somos necesarios* (*We're All Important*) (1956), and *El inquilino* (*The Tenant*) (1958). *El inquilino* was chosen to represent Spaih at the Edinburgh Film Festival but was stopped by a new member of the Housing Ministry from Extremadura, one of the poorest and least developed provinces in the country. The new bureaucrat denounced *El inquilino* as critical of official housing policies. The narrative was based on a true incident in which a family whose house was demolished was unable to find lodging. The film ends as the evicted family is being assisted by a group of workers.

When Nieves Conde protested the banning of his film, pointing out that it had already withstood the rigors of censorship, the minister of housing, José Luis Arrese, upheld the ban, explaining, "The good guys aren't wearing ties, and the bad guys are," an expression of fear of even a hint of populism.[9] A year later when *El inquilino* was re-released, the final sequence shows the evicted family driving in a bus to their new lodgings in an urban housing project called "La esperanza" (Hope).

If well-established conservative directors such as Nieves Conde encountered obstacles when trying to take a fresh approach, certainly Marco Ferreri, a young Italian who came to Spain in 1955 as coproducer of *Toro bravo,* felt harassed by censors when he made *El pisito (The Little Flat).* Based on a novel by Rafael Azcona, *El pisito* is set in postwar Barcelona. It stars two of Spain's rising talents, José Luis López Vásquez, later one of Saura's best male leads, and Mari Carillo. Another satire on the housing shortage, *El pisito* is a dark comedy in which a young man marries an eighty-year-old woman so that he and his fiancée can one day look forward to inheriting her apartment. When doña Martina dies, Rodolfo, rather than rushing his bride into their new home, is overcome with grief. Petrita, who has waited years to marry him, now considers marriage without enthusiasm. After years of loneliness and deprivation, life has passed these two patient people by and they no longer look forward to rewards which have come too late and at too great a cost.

Ferreri's next work, *El cochecito,* won the Film Critic's Award at the Venice Film Festival in 1960 and was chosen as best picture at the London Film Festival. It is another satire, this time on the lives of ordinary people. An elderly, bedridden man sees his friend living a full life with the use of an electric wheelchair. His family, however, cannot afford a *cochecito* for him, and he becomes depressed over his lack of independence. The inability to afford the benefits of modern technology began to embitter many Spaniards in an era when other Europeans were able to enjoy technological conveniences.

Marco Ferreri's career in the Spanish film industry was brief. While his films won honors abroad, they were heavily censored in Spain, both by cutting of scenes and by limited distribution. Acclaimed in Europe, Ferreri's Spanish films were seen only in second-rate theaters and by tiny audiences in their country of origin. Ferreri's residence permit was finally revoked and he was forced to return to Italy. His presence in Spain, however, lasted long enough to familiarize interested cinephiles with the latest techniques of Italian neorealism, a movement which heralded a new direction for Spanish film.

Censorship never flagged in its vigilance to prevent unseemly images from crossing the screens of Spain's public movie theaters. Private screens, however, were less accessible to state control, so that when, in 1950, a copy of Rossellini's *Open City* crossed the Spanish border in a diplomatic pouch to be viewed by a small group of film aficionados, new ideas in cinema entered Spain much the same way as the prohibited works of the French Enlightenment had managed to get into the hands of a few Spanish intellectuals in the eighteenth century.

In 1951, the year following *Open City's* surreptitious entry into Spain, the Institute of Italian Cultures held an Italian Film Week in Madrid. Film students at the National Film School were able to screen films that up to then had been banned, including Antonioni's *Chronicle of Love* (1950), De Sica's *Bicycle Thief* (1948) and *Miracle in Milan* (1951), Rossellini's *Open City* (1945) and *Paisá* (1946). No other event in the past fifteen years breathed life into Spanish cinema as did this event. Neorealist ideas began to be evident throughout the Spanish industry almost immediately, not only in works by young directors but in those by Franco loyalists such as Nieves Conde, who in *Surcos* showed Spaniards some of their first views of the seamy side of urban life.

Young directors saw neorealism as a way out of the sterile labyrinth of stereotypes that dominated Spanish film. Luis Berlanga recalls that the Italian Film Week was "decisive" in his career.[10] For his friend and collaborator, Juan Antonio Bardem, it was a turning point in which he saw the kind of films he would like to make.[11] The two worked together on *Bienvenido, Mr. Marshall* (*Welcome, Mr. Marshall*) (1952), a very popular film that introduced the Spanish public to an entirely new view of their country. Rather than glorifying past military exploits, *Mr. Marshall* was set in the present day in a small village whose peasants and town council are not heroes but ordinary people motivated by fear, greed, and self-interest as well as by community and national pride.

Four years later, in *Muerte de un ciclista* (*Death of a Cyclist*) (1956), Bardem stressed a critical view of Spain's comfortable bourgeoisie and included some brief scenes of the miserable living conditions of the poor. Marco Ferreri enlarged upon these scenes in *El pisito, Los chicos,* and *El cochecito,* so that social problems were not merely glimpsed in brief clips but became central themes in the films of these two directors.

The impact of neorealism was probably felt most by Carlos Saura. He recalls the shock of Spanish film students, prepared for their profession with study of *Isabel la Católica, Agustina de Aragón, and Catalina de Inglaterra,* when they realized that "se podía hacer cine en la calle y con gente normal" (you could make movies in the street with ordinary people).[12] Saura had always been interested in documentary, so the neorealist practice of using unknown actors and the perspective of collective rather than individual action appealed especially to him.

Saura's first full-length film, *Los golfos* (*The Drifters*) (1959), probably approaches neorealism more closely than any Spanish film of its time.

While insisting that *Los golfos* is not a neorealist film, Saura hedges, recalling that most of the cast were not professional actors but people who responded to an advertisement to act in the film. Among those chosen were two who could not read and who had to have their roles described to them.

In a conscious effort to avoid a closed ending, Saura, like some of the Italian neorealists, hoped to convey that the problems portrayed in *Los golfos* are not resolved and do not go away. The ending of the film was entirely accidental. The young Colombian matador refused to deliberately appear inept upon request, but he killed two bulls so inexpertly during the filming of the final scene that his performance corresponded exactly with the inevitable disaster envisioned by the director and required by the narrative.

Neorealist ideas were taken further by Saura than by any other young Spanish director. He compiled the script for *Los golfos* by assigning various parts of it to different writers and by using the result of this collaboration only as a possible outline of the action. He preferred to improvise most of the scenes and shot them on a very low budget in various lower-class neighborhoods of Madrid.

The infusion of new ideas from abroad generated such enthusiasm and desire for change among such a wide range of people that, four years after the Italian Film Week, the first public discussions of cinema were held in the ancient university town of Salamanca. Organized by Basilio Martín Patino and sponsored by the Cine Club Universitario (the Salamanca University Film Club) and the Sindicato Español Universitario (the Spanish Student Union) of Salamanca, the first Conversaciones Cinematográficas Nacionales attracted Spanish film professionals, critics, scholars, and writers representing a cross section of the ideological spectrum.

The Salamanca talks were held from May 14–19, 1955. An opening statement announcing the gathering set the tone for the talks. It was signed by Patino, Bardem, critic Muñoz Suay, and others who warned young Spanish hopefuls that if they were thinking of entering the film industry they should "volver a empezar"; that is, think again. "El cine español sigue siendo un cine de muñecas pintadas" (Spanish film continues to be a cinema of painted dolls). Neorealist influence is reflected in the announcement, as it complained that "el problema del cine español es que no tiene problemas, que no es testigo de nuestro tiempo" (the problem with Spanish film is that it has no problems, that it is not a witness to our time).[13] The announcement directly challenged censors to return to Spain's own tradition of Ribera, Goya, Quevedo, and Mateo Alemán. This remark referred to an ironic twist—censors had begun to ban from the screen some of Spain's greatest literary achievements. A film version of

Juan Ramón Jiménez's Nobel Prize—winning *Platero y yo,* a book of lyrical prose read by schoolchildren, was cancelled, and the filming of a play by Lope de Vega was opposed by censors as antimonarchical. (The pulling from a shop window of a reproduction of Goya's *Maja desnuda* by a Civil Guard already had become a national joke.)

Participants in the Salamanca talks brought with them a long list of demands, among the first of which was the codification of censorship criteria. Other topics discussed included protection quotas, distribution of films, and the establishment of a special category for films of particular artistic merit. The inclusion of a film professional on the Board of Censors was also called for as a minimum token of consideration for the film industry.

The talks concluded with a resounding condemnation of Spanish film by Juan Antonio Bardem. Like a revolutionary shout in the ears of the Franco government, Bardem's now famous "Five Points" statement was without equivocation: "Desde aquí, desde la Salamanca de Fray Luis de León y Unamuno, después de setenta años de cine, el cinema español es: políticamente, ineficaz; socialmente, falso; intelectualmente, ínfimo; estéticamente, nulo, e industrialmente, raquítico" (From here, from the Salamanca of Fray Luis de León and Unamuno, after seventy years of cinema, Spanish film is: politically, useless; socially, false; intellectually, inferior; esthetically, nonexistent, and industrially, sick).[14] From the heights of Franco's government a pardon, while not requested, was automatically extended for what was called "aquella especie de chiquillada" (that kind of childishness) and a warning issued about continuing in "this daring fashion."[15]

The Salamanca talks produced such a minuscule and delayed response that they were considered a failure by many who had supported them. Leftist groups criticized the talks as being an opportunity handed to the fascist government by a bourgeois group to sharpen its surveillance by codifying censorship criteria. The right wing declared the talks as evidence of Communist infiltration. For some, they were proof of the infancy of the Spanish film industry; for others, of its maturity. Their most important accomplishment was to have opened a dialogue on a national level about Spain's cinema and its future. A possible sign that, at the very least, the talks prompted some governmental insecurities was that, eleven months later, the administration's director general of theater and film was replaced by the ill-fated José Muñoz Fontán, whose career was later dismantled by *Viridiana.* The clearest indication of official response to the talks is the silence from the film industry that followed them. To the challenge raised by an oppressed but creative industry, the Franco government quietly turned its back.

In spite of the artistic vacuum created in Spain by censorship, the new ideas that managed to seep into the country were inspiring and being developed by young Spanish directors. The best of these included Juan Antonio Bardem and Luis García Berlanga. While it is idle to speculate upon what these two directors could have accomplished in ideal circumstances, they pioneered *la estética franquista,* the ironic film style which came to characterize Spanish film during the Franco period.

# 4. Juan Antonio Bardem

*El problema del franquismo era la impotencia por mostrar la realidad. Esa fue la dictadura cultural franquista, había que vencer a la censura.*

(The problem with *franquismo* was its inability to show reality. That was the Franco cultural dictatorship, censorship had to be overcome). —J. A. Bardem[1]

The son of theater actors, Bardem had an inherent feel for drama. He was born in Madrid on June 2, 1922, and was captivated from boyhood by the movies. His parents, Rafael Bardem and Matilde Muñoz Sampedro, hoped their son would enter a more stable profession. But Bardem persisted. He disguised his desire to be a movie director by telling his father he wanted to be a sound engineer. Someone told his father that such a career was impossible to study for in Spain, so Bardem found himself becoming an agronomist instead. In 1946, he began his professional career in the Film Department of the Ministry of Agriculture. The following year, however, when the Instituto de Investigaciones y Experiencias Cinematográficas (IIEC) opened its doors, Bardem was in its first class, where he met another aspiring director, Luis Berlanga. Bardem completed the film program only to have his final student project, entitled *Barajas, aereopuerto internacional* (Barajas, International Airport) rejected for unspecified "technical insufficiency." This phrase turned out to be a pretext for not adhering to the politics of the Franco autocrats; however, the lack of a diploma from the IIEC never seemed to be one of Bardem's obstacles. He began writing scripts with Berlanga such as *La Huida* and *El hombre vestido de negro*. The most important of these early scripts is *Esa pareja feliz.*

## Esa pareja feliz (That Happy Couple) (1951)

Spanish film at this time consisted of folkloric pieces, a few patriotic Civil War epics, and the stagy historical extravaganzas modeled after Hollywood, none of which bear any resemblance to contemporary life in Spain. So *Esa pareja feliz,* about an ordinary couple—Juan, who studies radio repair by correspondence and his wife, Carmen, who takes in sewing—is unusual simply for reflecting the daily life of the average Spaniard in 1951. Juan loses money when he sinks his savings into a get-rich-quick scheme and his partner disappears with the cash. He finds that his radio repair diploma is worth nothing when he can barely put his first repair job back together. Humiliated and broke, he and Carmen live by the naive faith that with hard work, patience, and being good citizens they will one day be rich and happy.

Carmen, an avid reader of slick magazines, enters and wins a publicity contest. A company offers one day of luxury to the winners, who are designated "The Happy Couple of the Day." For twenty-four hours they have all they have dreamed of—a car, shopping at fine stores, meals at restaurants, and a night on the town. But for Juan, who does not know how to dance, the night club is no fun. Like a pair of Cinderellas their dream soon ends and they are back in their cramped flat. Juan and Carmen now realize that a future of wealth and comfort will be forever out of reach for them and for an entire class of people who toil for material joys they will never realize. Disillusioned, they resign themselves to what the camera reveals as miserable living conditions and a life of hard labor. At the same time they resolve not to give up the struggle to improve their condition. Juan and Carmen learn the bitter lesson that, for unskilled workers, a society whose only rewards are material benefits is inaccessible and irrelevant.

In 1952, Bardem collaborated with Berlanga on the script of *Bienvenido, Mr. Marshall*. But he was nearly bankrupt and had to sell his interest in the project and return for a time to his old job at the Ministry of Agriculture. When *Bienvenido* won a Critic's Prize in Cannes, Bardem bought a third-class train ticket to Cannes, his first visit out of the country. His first film entirely of his own effort is *Cómicos*.

## Cómicos (Actors) (1953)

*Cómicos* remains unique in Spanish cinema history. It was the first of a still small group of Spanish films in which a protagonist is an intelligent, attractive, professional female who, of her own choice, prefers to remain single and pursue her career. Bardem was inspired by Manckiewicz's *All about Eve* in treating this theme. The director's cousin Conchita serves as the model for the central character, Ana Ruiz, who at twenty-five has been a member of a touring theatrical company for four years and is tired of waiting for her chance to succeed. Ana introduces us to the other actors: the troupe's owners, doña Carmen and don Antonio, Marga, Miguel, and the stage manager. We see the grueling life a touring company leads—trains to catch at three and four in the morning to be in the next town in time to go on stage. They stay in cheap hotels without ever enough time to visit the towns they travel through or enjoy their surroundings. Marga ridicules the parts they get:

MARGA: *Alta comedia: "¡Ja! ¡Ja! ¿Este Pachín es imponente, . . . imponente, verdad, Adelaida?" Comedia para reir y para llorar: "¡Ni un momento más; no estaré ni un momento más! ¡Ud. no es mi padre!" Comedia andaluza: "¡Osu! ¡Cómo estaba la iglesia! ¡Toda cuajadita de flores! ¡Ay, chiquiyo, misamente paresía que la Virgen yoraba! ¡Digo!"*
ANA: *¿Qué se puede hacer?*
MARGA: *Emigrar.*

(MARGA: High drama: "Ha! Ha! This cad is fresh, don't you think, Adelaida?" Tragicomedy: "I won't stay another minute! You are not my father!" Andalusian drama: "Oh, gracious. You should have seen the church! All decorated with flowers! Honey child, it seemed like the Virgin herself was crying! I declare!"
ANA: What can you do?
MARGA: Emigrate.)

Miguel has joined the company in hopes that he can win Ana, but he, too, has had enough. He is going back to his village and asks Ana to come with him. She has no trouble making up her mind, and Miguel tells her she loves the theater more than she does him. "It's different . . . How can I explain?" but he gets off the train without her and does not look back.

A playwright reads his new play to the troupe and Ana is sure that the leading female role is for her. When she learns that doña Carmen, in spite of her age, retains the young protagonist's role for herself, she is furious. In retribution, Ana wanders silently across the stage during one of doña Carmen's performances. Ana is so desperate that she goes out with Marga and her friend Pepe. They introduce her to Carlos, a theater impresario who offers her star billing in a company he says he is forming. Ana almost accepts before she learns that Carlos is a collector of lead actresses. She vacillates. She is unknown, without opportunity or even the possibility of better offers.

When the new play opens it is a stunning success. The next night, doña Carmen is too fatigued to go on stage. The play is a sellout, but the doctor refuses to allow doña Carmen out of the hospital. The theater owner refuses to cancel to a sold-out public. Ana has her chance. She is so frightened she cannot remember any of the lines, but once on stage she amazes the troupe with her skill. The audience is spellbound. After the crowd has left, Carlos tells her condescendingly, "Daddy is proud of you." Ana decides that she can now do without Carlos and tells him to leave. At this point, don Antonio congratulates her and also tells her that doña Carmen has recovered and will want her part back the next night.

Ana is still transfixed by her success and stands on stage looking at the empty theater. Later, as the train pulls out for the next town, she stares at "a point into the unknown future." Strangely, Ana seems more satisfied since she has proven herself to be the professional she knew she was. She feels part of the troupe rather than only an untried bit-part player. Now she is confident about her future.

*Cómicos* was also a testing ground for its director. Berlanga was now winning accolades for *Bienvenido, Mr. Marshall* as well as being given the credit for the success of *Esa pareja feliz.* So Bardem, like Ana, had to convince the public of his talent. He chose to introduce Ana both as narrator and participant in the film, a stylistic complexity new to Spanish film. *Cómicos* was praised not only for its excellent dialogue but for presenting a fresh approach to narrative development.

### Felices Pascuas (Merry Christmas) (1954)

Bardem is not at home in comedy, so his next film was another trial for him. His characters, Juan and Pilar, are like the couple of *Esa pareja feliz,* workers looking for an easy road to riches. This time it is Juan who wins a lottery prize but who is by now embittered by his lack of opportunity. He goes home to find that Pilar has won a lamb in a contest. Juan looks at the lamb and sees Christmas Eve dinner, but the lamb is winning the hearts of his family. When the day to prepare dinner arrives, no one has the will to lay a hand on Bolita.

While the lamb is outside, gypsies steal it and leave it in a breadbasket which is being sent to a convent. A soldier steals it from the basket and leaves it near a commercial truck. The truck's drivers toss Bolita into a load of sheep headed for slaughter. Juan follows the lamb's odyssey, rescues it, and takes it home, where his family dances with joy to have their pet back. Bolita has come to represent humility, which Juan lacked. But, in his search for Bolita, Juan learns to understand and even to share his family's affection for the innocent creature. Bolita has enlarged Juan's humanity.

In *Felices Pascuas,* Bardem tries to recycle some of the motifs of *Esa pareja feliz.* He ridicules the innocent, naive Spanish worker who often waits for solutions to his problems to drop from nowhere. He also experiments with characters as symbols—the gypsies representing Spain, the soldier as the military establishment, and Bolita as the spirit of humility and cooperation. But none of the film's messages is very clear. Bardem's use of symbolic figures, one of his favorite techniques, is the stylistic device for which he has been most consistently criticized. He leaves untouched the humorous possibilities of *Felices Pascuas* and concentrates instead on the development of Juan's character from disillusioned worker to humane father and husband. In his zeal to stress a moral lesson, Bardem neglects the visual style and narrative content of *Felices Pascuas.*

Juan Antonio Bardem, *Muerte de un ciclista* (1956).

### Muerte de un ciclista (Death of a Cyclist) (1955)

This is the film that brought Bardem international acclaim and is still considered among his best. It is a courageous analysis of the social indifference of a complacent bourgeoisie. The characters are entirely credible and the cinematography is fresh and dramatic. María José (Lucía Bose), a married woman, is driving her lover, Juan, a university professor, back into town one afternoon when she accidentally runs over and kills a cyclist. Juan (Alberto Closas) wants to report the incident. María José, fearing publicity about the incident and refusing to face her guilt, prefers to forget about it. Juan is seen through the wheel of the bicycle running toward the victim. The incident causes an immediate chill between the two lovers and they continue their drive in silence.

The protagonists' social environment is observed in scenes of a party attended by wealthy Spanish conservatives and an inevitable pair of rich Americans. Juan, like Bardem himself at one time, is a mathematics instructor. He is trying to secure a university chair and, his mother reminds him, he has a powerful brother-in-law who could help him. But Juan, haunted by the death of the cyclist, is going through a *crise de conscience*. His alienation from bourgeois society becomes clear in a scene at the racetrack. He joins María José there to watch horses train and is stunned

Juan Antonio Bardem, *Muerte de un ciclista* (1956).

when someone reads in the newspaper a notice announcing the cyclist's death. The well-to-do racing fans, amused by the article, laugh at it while Juan suffers in silent humiliation.

The guilt-ridden Juan now becomes a compulsive newspaper reader, watching for further details of the cyclist's death. A long shot of his classroom reveals him engrossed in his paper while one of his students, Mathilde, is presenting a complicated formula on the blackboard. Not having heard her arguments, he suspends her for "insufficient preparation," the vague cliché given to Bardem himself when he was refused a diploma from IIEC. Juan faces an angry Mathilde in his office. "You don't have to worry, you have your brother-in-law who is very powerful. But I am alone," she retorts, thus pointing out the inequality of a system that tolerates professorial incompetence while blaming students.

Students mount a protest rally in support of Mathilde, although it is Juan who feels more and more alone. María José only wants to escape from responsibility, while Juan balks at blatant power politics, such as calling on his brother-in-law. Public scandal looms over them when, at a party, a repulsive art critic, Rafa, gets drunk and accuses Juan of *cosas sucias* (dirty things) with María José. When she confronts Rafa, he tells her that he saw her in a car with "that man." Rafa, further enraged when María José's husband defends her, throws a bottle through a window.

Window shots seem especially enticing to Bardem—in this film there are three of them. The shot of a bottle crashing through the window is used to dramatize jealousy and conflict. An oval church window frames the face of María José, underlining the irony of the lovers' secret meeting in a church. During the student protest, Mathilde visits Juan's office again and they observe the action through a window that is fractured by a rock tossed by one of the students. Windows are the protective shield through which the protagonists have observed life, but Juan's is cracking badly. Ashamed of suspending Mathilde and of his own lack of courage, Juan now hands Mathilde an envelope containing his resignation from his teaching position. When he informs María José of his decision, she, lacking Juan's resolve to admit mistakes, takes refuge in ignorance and exaggerated femininity: "It's too complicated for a woman like me," she complains and prepares to leave with her husband, who has had enough and is going away.

It is raining when Juan and María José go for their last ride together. As the car heads into the camera, windshield wipers create a nervous rhythm in this final scene. Juan reminds her they are driving down the same road "where we killed. . . ." They stop on the deserted highway to take a walk. Dismal fields surround them. María José, very tense, gets back in the car, turns the key, starts the engine. In her panic she loses control over the car and runs over Juan. She speeds down the dark, slick road and swerves to miss another cyclist. This time her car, white sidewalls flashing in the darkness, careens off the highway and crashes. The camera closes in on her body, hanging upside down in the wreckage. The cyclist pedals for help toward a nearby store. In its window there is a light. The film closes with a long shot of the window illuminating the night, perhaps a hopeful sign of Spain searching in a sea of darkness.

At a time when the problems of postwar social commitment and moral responsibility were being debated in Europe by Sartre and Camus, Bardem was one of the few film directors in Spain willing to dispense with the stale genres of falsified history and folkore. *Muerte de un ciclista* modernizes Spanish cinema. It restores Spanish film to an international level of discourse by unmasking social conformity and indicting a comfortable but socially illiterate bourgeoisie. *Muerte de un ciclista* also sets another pattern in Spanish film history. While daring directors such as Buñuel and Marco Ferreri were lauded elsewhere, they were harassed in Spain. Although *Muerte de un ciclista* won awards abroad (the Critic's Prize at Cannes), at home it was so disturbing that Bardem, during the shooting of his next film, was arrested.

### Calle mayor (Main Street) (1956)

Bardem's critique of Spain's problems in his films had brought him under close scrutiny by the Franco regime. He does not know why he was arrested shortly after he had begun to film *Calle mayor,* but his crew refused to work without him and, apparently to avoid adverse international publicity, he was soon released. *Calle mayor* was exhibited at the Venice Festival in 1956 under the protest of the Spanish Ministry of Information, which required a disclaimer to be included in the film saying that events described in it "could happen in any country." The fact is, however, that *Calle mayor* is based on the Spanish play *La señorita de Trevélez* (1916) by Carlos Arniches and had already been adapted for the screen in 1935, when a film version of it was directed by Edgar Neville. So Bardem only adapted what was already recognized as one of Spain's most accurate dramatic portraits of provincial life and one of the outstanding plays in modern Spanish theater. Like the Civil Guards, who required that the picture of Goya's *Maja desnuda* be removed from a provincial Spanish store window, the Franco regime began to censor Spain's own best works of art.

The film's title is taken from the main street which is used throughout Hispanic towns and villages for the custom of *paseándose,* taking an evening stroll to see and be seen. But the protagonist, Isabel, is thirty-five, an age at which Spanish ladies not yet married were expected to gracefully drop out of the marriage market and silently declare themselves unmarriageable. Isabel breaks this unspoken rule and continues to *pasearse* and to enjoy the company of her younger friends. So the town dandies decide that they should teach Isabel a lesson. They choose one of their number, Juan, to pretend affection for her, become her steady boyfriend, or *novio,* and then, on the night of the town fiesta at the casino, to abandon her.

Isabel falls for the scheme and accepts Juan's attentions. Her friend from Madrid, Federico, warns her of the scheme and advises her to leave town. At first humiliated, Isabel plans to follow his advice. But she realizes that this is her home and refuses to be driven out, since she has no possible life elsewhere. A native of the town, Isabel dreamed of becoming a stewardess, but this profession, like that of a sound engineer, was out of reach of provincial aspirants.

Characters such as Juan are seen as the natural result of an empty, grotesque, and cruel way of life. Entirely isolated and complacent, young men of the provinces lead a stultifying existence drinking at the Miami Bar and enjoying abusive jokes in an endless display of macho behavior. Life offers provincial females a more nurturing but equally boring series of masses and rosaries, charity events, and domestic chores. Apparently the primary social contact between the two sexes is on the *calle mayor.* This social pattern has produced the kind of abyss between men and women that allows Juan to join village churls in deceiving Isabel, and that leaves Isabel staring at the rain through a window in the final scene.

## La venganza (Vengeance) (1957)

*La venganza* was to have been a great epic entitled *The Reapers*, the first of a series Bardem planned on the lives of Spanish working men and women, including coalminers and fishermen. The film's voice-off narration introduced into Spanish film an analogy of Spanish farm workers with those of other countries, an international view of labor entirely new to Spanish film and highly suspect to Spanish censors:

> *Todos los años cuando el trigo está maduro, llegan hasta las dos Castillas los hombres de Galicia, Extremadura, Cuenca, de las tierras altas de Andalucía. Es una emigración temporal de gente de pastos, olivar, o viñas, donde la labor en esa época es nula, a la llanura, donde el trigo es mucho, y los brazos, pocos. Es un fenómeno que se hermana con el de los hombres y mujeres de las "risaias" del Po, las gentes valencianas que suben hasta las tierras de la Camarga, los "pickers" que llegan desde Oklahoma a California, los "espaldas mojadas" mexicanos que atraviesan el rio Colorado.*

> (Every year when the wheat is ripe, men from Galicia, Extremadura, Cuenca, and from the highlands of Andalusia go to the two provinces of Castile. It is a seasonal migration of people from the pastures, vineyards, and olive groves where there is no work this time of year to the plains, where there is much wheat and few arms to gather it. It is a phenomenon related to that of the men and women of the "risaias" of the Po, the Valencians who go up to the lands of the Camargue, the "pickers" who go from Oklahoma to California, and the Mexican wetbacks who cross the Colorado [sic] River.)

The action of *La venganza* centers around a family feud. Juan Díaz returns from serving a ten-year jail sentence for a crime he did not commit. He has sworn to his sister Andrea to settle this injustice with Luis, the real criminal and the last member of the town's failing aristocracy, which has inhabited the local hacienda for centuries.

Juan participates in a strike with local day workers, hoping to force landowners to pay better wages for their work. Their victory, however, goes up in flames when the crop catches fire and burns the parched fields. The reapers fear mechanization in the field and share aging Santiago's anger when the old man is wounded trying to match his strength against that of a tractor.

Bardem hoped to use reapers instead of actors in *La venganza* but was prohibited from doing so. Still, the worn, wrinkled faces of the actors lend an authenticity that the merry peasants of earlier, conformist folklore films never projected. Puppeteers, wandering musicians, landowners, and even the village idiot make the characters appear to derive from the Spanish tradition of the picaresque novel.

Censors were especially wary of the proletarian context of *La venganza*. They required the time of the film's action to be set back from 1958 to 1931 so as to make the reapers' strike appear to have happened during the Second Republic rather than the Franco regime. Bardem was also made to change the title of the film from *Los segadores* (*The Reapers*), the title of a popular song of opposition to the government, to *La venganza*. With the title change, emphasis thus shifted from the workers to the family feud and love story. Bardem lamented, "Mi idea era hacer ese gran fresco del mundo del trabajo español . . . y se quedó en un melodrama" (I wanted to make a great world fresco of Spanish labor . . . and it remained a melodrama).[2]

Yet *La venganza* rises above melodrama. The choice of workers as central figures reveals the director's debt to great social films such as *Potemkin,* Dovzhenko's *La Ligne général,* and De Santis's *Giorni d'amore.* Juan, the peasant unjustly punished, returns to his country like the many political exiles who returned after the Civil War to an authoritarian, triumphal regime. Luis, scion of a decadent aristocracy, now shares the peasants' poverty. Andrea, Juan's sister, works with the economic and social reality faced by all Spanish women—that of being bound to the past with opportunities closed for the future. It is Andrea, however, who releases Juan from the vengeance they had sworn together. As the feuding men draw knives in the final sequence, Andrea stands between them and announces, "La tierra es grande y todos cabemos en ella" (The land is wide and we all have a place in it). Her love for Luis dissolves the feud and announces the theme of reconciliation which Bardem proposes as essential for national unity.

This conciliatory tone did not appease the censors, who dismantled not only *La venganza* but Bardem's entire creative life for the next decade. Rather than proceeding with his plan for a series of workers' epics, he made instead three mediocre films: *Sonatas* (1959), based on two decadent prose works by Ramón Valle-Inclán; *A las cinco de la tarde* (1960), revealing corruption in the world of bullfighting; and *Los inocentes* (1962), a study of love and conformity in the industrial ruling class of Guipúzcoa in the Basque country. In 1960 Bardem had written *Nunca pasa nada,* but that was the year of *Viridiana.* Buñuel's return to Spain and his triumph and accompanying scandal rocked the shaky world of Spanish cinema (see Chapter 7) so that *Nunca pasa nada* was not just censored but prohibited altogether. Not until 1963 was it possible to make this film, which many critics consider Bardem's best. With its inventory of his consistent themes of stagnation and hypocrisy (*Calle ma-*

*yor*), ignorance (*Felices Pascuas*), and social complacency (*Muerte de un ciclista*), *Nunca pasa nada* is certainly Bardem's most representative film.

### *Nunca pasa nada (Nothing Ever Happens)* (1963)

An aging tourist bus makes an unscheduled stop in a rural village while bringing a young French tourist, Jackie, to a doctor. The bus lurches on its way, leaving Jackie at the hospital for an appendectomy. As the doctor, Enrique, performs the operation, the camera focuses on a village street where we see three women wearing black lace mantillas returning from mass. The camera follows Julia, Enrique's wife, as she does some shopping. In the pharmacy she hears the latest gossip: *una francesa* is in town, is in the hospital, and probably, one of the gossips speculates, is "desnuda frente al doctor" (nude in front of the doctor).

As modern physicians go, Enrique does seem to spend an inordinate amount of post-op time at his patient's bedside. But a cut to Enrique's own bedroom as he and Julia get ready for bed that evening explains why. He and Julia apparently stopped talking to each other some time ago. She asks about his new patient, he mumbles a few syllables, and they get into bed, lying rigidly side by side. No touching. So, when he accidentally overturns Jackie's suitcase the next morning in the hospital and discovers undies among her clothes, dark music begins, announcing Enrique's midlife rediscovery of sensuality. But a nun enters and the music stops.

Jackie's recovery is miraculously swift. The doctor finds her dancing in her room on his next visit. He offers to find her a room in a friend's home where, he tells her, she'll be more comfortable, meaning without the nuns. The next scene is of Jackie at the rural farm auction, where all the humans and most of the mules and pigs stare at their blonde, well-built visitor, played with an almost comic sense of timing by French actress Corinne Marchand. Her only friend is Juan (Jean-Pierre Cassell) the local French teacher and poet.

But Juan, who tutors Julia's children, is in love with Julia. Jackie counsels him to leave town, sensible advice since Julia is too respectable to seriously consider taking a lover. Enrique, fifty-one and finding his life stale, is depressed and thinks only of Jackie. He ignites town gossip by taking her hunting and staying with her overnight at an inn. When Julia finds out she is furious and demands a separation.

One night Jackie is so bored that, to amuse herself, she goes to a bar and dances, at first by herself. A circle of gaping peasants gathers and she invites one of them to dance. Enrique passes by and sees this as an unseemly display. In his fury he becomes the typical jealous, abusive, raging macho. Jackie responds by paying him for the operation and taking the next bus out of town. She kisses Juan good-bye and leaves the outraged doctor fulminating at the bus station.

The final scene is the film's best. Julia comes by, takes the bewildered Enrique's arm, and leads him off. The camera follows them, focusing on a traffic sign in the background whose arrow points to the right. Now the camera faces them as they keep walking straight ahead. They have taken the wrong direction in life, have failed to negotiate necessary changes. Representatives of the rigid morality of their village and of Spanish culture in general, in which divorce was illegal until 1978, Julia and Enrique have no choice. Staring marital disaster in the face, they walk directly into it, miserable, repressed, resigned.

It is impossible to know what effect state manipulation has had on Bardem's creativity, whether what Manuel Summers termed the constant *toreando* (bullfighting) with the censor has forged Bardem's films into being more concise, more subtle than they would otherwise have been. One possible answer is his post-Franco *Siete días en enero* (1978), discussed in the final chapter. But after *Nunca pasa nada* Bardem entered a creative decline in which the strong voice of social consciousness so central to his best works falls silent. He realized he faced an impasse when *Nunca pasa nada* was not received well in Cannes.

By 1963, European culture was changing swiftly, while in Spain things remained the same. Bardem decided that "mis posibilidades actualmente, son hacer cine extranjero en España" (my possibilities are to make foreign film in Spain).[3] He spent the late 1960s and early 1970s doing just that: *Los pianos mecánicos* (1966), *Varietés* (1970), and *La corrupción de Chris Miller* (1972) are coproduced vehicles for international stars. In 1976 he made another attempt at social commentary, *El puente* (*The Bridge*), about a motorcycle mechanic who discovers that there is more to life and to himself than searching for the perfect female body. *El puente* reveals a director who has lost control and balance so that bad jokes and ridiculous situations bear no relation to a didactic message and ending. Repetitive long shots of the motorcycle, the film's unifying sign, heading down the highway seem to serve primarily as time fillers.

Bardem's misfortune was to have been suddenly lionized by French film critics excited over *Muerte de un ciclista* and then just as suddenly attacked by them, especially by Truffaut. César Santos Fontenla best describes Bardem's dilemma in terms of Spain's cultural contradictions. Bardem knew he must make Spanish film speak to an international audience. But, "en un país de subdesarrollo cultural como es el nuestro es poco menos que imposible realizar una obra que, al tiempo que . . . valga para nuestro mercado, sirva para el exterior" (in a culturally undeveloped country like ours it is little less than impossible to direct a film that, at the same time that it wins our market, . . . works abroad as well).[4] He continued to search for the right film language that would be understood both in Spain and in Europe. But what appears to a Spanish public as a cold critical eye reflects clearly Spain's social problems to Europeans. His efforts to create popular films for a Spanish audience (*Sonatas* and *La venganza*) failed miserably abroad.

If Bardem never found just the right cinematic language with which to speak to both cultures, neither, as Fontenla remarks, did Spain, meaning that it is impossible to judge Spain's directors outside their peculiar national context. Bardem's voice of protest was, with its undeniable intellectual ring, too advanced for the general Spanish public. His one-time collaborator, Luis Berlanga, comes closer to creating a national cinema than Bardem. It was Bardem, however, who first defined the abysmal state of Spanish cinema. His films are a continuation of this effort and are the first serious attempt to awaken the national social consciousness.

# 5. Luis García Berlanga

Luis García Berlanga, who began his career with Bardem, shares his colleague's attempts to challenge the Franco myth yet with an opposite, comic mode of discourse. While Bardem requires his audiences to reflect upon his generally somber narratives, Berlanga disarms his public with laughter while ridiculing Spanish political situations and social types. Bardem's orderly, well-made plots and carefully constructed sets contrast sharply with Berlanga's chaotic farces, whose rapid pace has had two characters delivering lines at the same time. Berlanga refers to this confusion as his *barroquismo valenciano* (Valencian baroque),[1] a style which helps create an atmosphere in which his outrageous visual gags are possible. Berlanga's satire reveals sharp social commentary aimed at his favorite targets, women and the abuse of power. The director describes his range of personal and social attitudes by saying that "como persona soy cristiano, como creador, anarquista, y como súbdito, liberal" (personally, I'm a Christian, creatively, an anarchist, and politically, liberal) (p. 25).

Luis Berlanga, born in Valencia to a family of small shopkeepers in July 1921, had, like Buñuel, a Jesuit upbringing. When the order was expelled from Spain in 1931, Berlanga was sent briefly to school in Switzerland. Never studious, he sold his textbooks to watch Marlene Dietrich movies and published poems to Ingrid Bergman in Valencia newspapers. Too young to fight in the Civil War, Berlanga volunteered in 1940 for the fascist División Azul that went to the Soviet Union to aid the Nazi cause. Berlanga's reasons for joining this unit range from noble (to save his liberal father from a death sentence) to more practical (to avoid later compulsory military duty). The experience was grueling and left in him an indelible fear of death which may account for the comic treatment of death and lack of violence in his early films.

Berlanga's career, which spans three decades from 1951 to the present, consists of four periods of activity followed by three to four idle years. This pattern of ebb and flow has caused some critics to complain that Berlanga is lazy and works only when he wants. Yet a collection of some thirty unpublished scripts suggests that Berlanga's inactivity has neither been voluntary nor unproductive.

Ten years after his first film, Berlanga began a collaboration with scriptwriter Rafael Azcona that has lasted until the present. Azcona's influence on Berlanga is considered to have sharpened the director's critical mind and to have brought order and focus to his intuitive, spontaneous narratives. *Plácido* (1961) was their first collaborative effort, followed by *El verdugo* (1963), considered Berlanga's best film. But before meeting Azcona, Berlanga had defined his own personality clearly with the unconventional and very popular *Bienvenido, Mr. Marshall*.

### Bienvenido, Mr. Marshall (Welcome, Mr. Marshall) (1952)

This remarkable film, written in collaboration with Bardem and the well-known comic dramatist Miguel Mihura, breaks with the conventions of Spanish film in the 1950s and opens new horizons for the future. Neither a heroic nor a historical extravaganza, *Bienvenido* treats political events of the day—the exclusion of Spain from Marshall Plan funds. It was not filmed in a studio but in a village, Guadalix de la Sierra; its protagonist is neither a heroic individual nor of patriotic or military virtue but the Spanish populace, represented by the village of Villar del Río. The fact that the visiting delegate confuses the town's name, calling it Villar del Campo, indicates that it is indistinguishable from any other ordinary Spanish village. A voice-off introduces the village and its citizens—the aging mayor, who wears a hearing aid; the priest; the schoolteacher, Eloisa; don Emiliano, the doctor; and don Luis, the typical Spanish nobleman who inherited opinions but no money from illustrious predecessors.

Rural life in Villar del Río is uneventful until the general delegate, accompanied by three assistants dressed in black and carrying briefcases, arrives at the town hall. The delegate, in formal attire, tells the mayor that "los Americanos del norte, los del plan Marshall," will visit the village soon. He advises the mayor to speak "desde el balcón" (from the balcony). "¿De qué?" (About what?) "De la industria." (About industry.) "¿De qué industria? (What industry?) With the mention of industry, the conversation closes. This was recognizable to Spaniards as a mild joke on the economic lethargy of the Franco government. The delegate and his assistants stride out and depart with don Pablo, the mayor, having to remind him of the correct name of the village.

The comedy centers upon villagers' reactions to the news that Americans are coming. The visiting flamenco singer, Carmen, and her promoter, Manolo, agree to organize their welcome. The priest is suspicious and begins to sermonize. "El mal nos manda sus mensajeros" (Evil is sending us its messengers). His enumerations of America's sins include references to ancient Spanish religious taboos: fifty million Protestants, millions of Jews, and a million divorces. But the mayor, don Pablo, sees reports on No-Do of American largess to Italy—tractors and other equipment—and decides to go all out to win some for his people. That night, the short rotund mayor practices oratory in front of a mirror dressed in his nightshirt and beret.

A frenzy possesses the town. When a tractor and a road-smoother roll down the main street decorated with American flags, people run out shouting, "The Americans are here." The mayor begins in his best oratorical style: "O noble pueblo americano," to which the tractor driver responds that they are only a road crew doing repairs and carrying flags in case the Americans see them.

The town council meeting is a hilarious response of Spanish minds to a new challenge. Elaborate plans for town beautification are discussed. While the doctor explains how a spout can be added to the fountain in the plaza someone comes in to spray for flies and talk turns instead to the flamenco singer, Carmen, and her legs. The nobleman opposes any reception for the visitors. Later he appears at the mayor's public speech and asks his fellow villagers one of the important questions of the film: "¿Qué esperan de esta piñata?" (What do you expect from this piñata?). In answer to this question, the townspeople, told that they can ask for one thing, line up, like children visiting Santa Claus, and record their wish—a bridle, a rifle, a clarinet, a bicycle. A man who at first says he wants nothing changes his mind and says, "A stereoscope." Two women who ask for a sewing machine fight over who had the idea first.

One of the innovations of the film is the visualization of images that pass through the villagers' heads as they dream of what they really meant to request. Instead of dreams, don Cosme, the suspicious priest, has nightmares of being led to judgment by members of the infamous House Un-American Activities Committee marching, as in a Holy Week procession, garbed in black hoods with "KKK" emblazoned on the back of black robes. A peasant dreams of an American plane flying overhead with three bearded men inside dropping gifts out the door. They are the Three Wise Men, although one is in naval uniform, another is dressed like Santa Claus. They salute and drop a box that turns out to be a tractor, which the peasants climb onto and drive away. The nobleman, don Luis, dreams of the discovery and conquest of America in which he, a conquistador, is captured and eaten by Indians. This is one of the few references in Spanish film of the 1950s to an ignominious rather than a noble national past. The most elaborate dream is the mayor's. Lying in bed with his beret on, don Pablo dreams a spoof of an American Western bar scene, complete with chorus girls and shoot-out.

The central character of don Pablo, the mayor, serves to unify *Bien-*

*venido*. He is portrayed as an incomparable old bungler by José (Pepe) Isbert. Isbert's portly body, arms waving, enlivens almost any scene. His spoof of the American sheriff and of the Spanish mayor is a remarkable attempt to demystify stereotypes of authority. Berlanga, who prefers not to direct his actors but rather expects them to improvise their lines, came to rely often on the highly professional talents of Pepe Isbert.

*Bienvenido* is a friendly satire, not only of Spanish manners and characters but of American stereotypes as well. The short Spanish mayor makes the Western sheriff look like a clown in oversized Western hat and pistols. His enemy is the promoter and their conflict is seen in terms of the duel of the American Old West. Their behavior mocks the Western hero: they drink, spit, slide glasses up and down the bar, and start a fight that has the bartender hiding. In the ensuing general brawl, the mayor falls to the floor in fear but recovers when he views Carmen's leg and begins caressing it. Unfortunately, the leg turns out to be a table leg as the old man wakes from his dream.

Berlanga is the only Spanish filmmaker to attempt to focus upon current political issues as central themes. The safest approach to national trauma was comedy that ridiculed but also expressed underlying frustrations and illusions of the Spanish people. The arrival of the Americans turns out to be only a swift passage of their caravan through town. The disappointed villagers must now pay for the flamenco costumes they rented and feel the sting of having their fondest wishes ignored. The film ends with shots of the reality of their lives—cows, plowing, field-workers, the clear sky overhead. The experience has revealed that like most people the Spanish villagers believed for a moment in Santa Claus.

Berlanga's talent for visual gags in *Bienvenido* is another rich source of laughs. His gallery of village representatives lends itself to caricature so that Spanish types are distorted into slapstick proportion in the dream sequences. Don Luis, the grumpy nobleman sailing in his boat, "Purita," (Purity), represents a spoof of the penniless conquistador. Fakery acquires a Spanish flavor when the villagers wall up a bull so that only its head shows above a sign identifying it as the famous bull killed by Manolete. The Old West torch song becomes barely recognizable in Carmen's flamenco version of it in the saloon scene. The camera generally views these characters in long shots to emphasize their status as parts of the fabric of national life. This tender, funny, at times poignant group portrait is as close as Spanish film comes to rendering the national reality of the 1950s.

## Calabuch (1956)

While the script and idea of *Calabuch* are not Berlanga's, the film is characteristic of his early approach to national problems as a gently satiric comedy of manners. It is a sympathetic sketch of an American scientist, Jorge Hamilton, who flees the United States so as not to have to make atom bombs. Hamilton wanders down the beach to the seaside village of Calabuch, a name chosen by the director for its *resonancia mediterránea*. Calabuch, population 928, is a rural Spanish paradise where the local Civil Guards, smugglers, lighthouse keepers, priest, and schoolteacher share a dirt-poor but harmonious existence in blissful isolation from the world. The village is seen in a long shot surrounded by hills crowned by a castle and cradled in a small beach cove.

This idyllic setting contrasts sharply with the rocket seen blasting off in the newsreels, which announce the disappearance of a famous scientist in the early frames of the film. The camera focuses on plump American actor Edmund Gwyn, who stars as Jorge. He approaches the village and is suddenly met by a ridiculous marching militia. The soldiers are dressed in Roman garb and carry lances, a visual joke suggesting that Spanish provincial armies may be antique in the world of modern armaments but, unlike the rocket, at least pose no global threat.

Jorge finds his way to Calabuch and befriends the villagers. They welcome him as a good-natured *vagabundo* whose talents soon make him a valuable member of the community. The local fiesta is enhanced by his advanced fireworks displays and he even plays the organ for a wedding, ending the ceremony with a loud version of *Oh! Susanna*. Berlanga enjoys laughing at local types, such as the travelling torero whose bullring is a barricade of empty boats at the seashore. The brave bull named Boca Negra looks like a Jersey cow and chases the torero into the surf. The corrida ends when darkness falls and the bull lies down to sleep, covered with a blanket by his loving master. In the early hours before dawn, the torero begs the bull to get up so they can get on the road.

Berlanga also ridicules another Spanish form of entertainment, the No-Do—obligatory movie newsreels shown during the *franquista* period. The local smuggler is the projectionist who explains that No-Do is hopelessly out of date—"Sólo procesiones, bicicletas, nada que pasa en el mundo" (Just parades, bicycles, nothing that's happening in the world). A title flashes on screen: "Vida nacional," followed by another, "Ceremonia militar." We see a rocket blasting off, then a quick shot of Jorge before the projector blows up.

One day ships are sighted in the bay. The villagers, who suspect their talented visitor's identity, receive the message, "Prepare to deliver Jorge." The town council meets to plot its course. An inventory of weapons turns up a gun and an antique cannon. A rare laugh at the military is allowed in this visual jest at Spain's lack of modern weaponry. An army tent is raised in the plaza to the accompaniment of martial music and a map is drawn. A helicopter appears overhead, bringing with it fear that the American fleet "van a dejar caer una bomba atómica" (is going to drop an atomic bomb). (This prophetic scene came close to realization ten years later when a U.S. atomic warhead was lost off the coast of Palomares in the winter of 1966.) The villagers offer Jorge a place to hide but the scientist warns them that there is no such place. Church bells toll as Jorge walks slowly past the Roman militia assembled on the beach and heads toward the waiting launch. The admirals' fear that Jorge will reveal atomic secrets seems preposterous as the villagers set off next year's fireworks display in honor of their departing guest and the military helicopter rises over the medieval castle on the hill.

Although *Calabuch* is a farce it reflects the conflict between the Spanish people's distrust of technology and their country's close military alliance with the United States which was being forged by Franco in the 1950s. The sleepy village is Berlanga's metaphor for Spain in the world of modern warfare—militarily ineffectual but whose position on the margin of world events makes the country seem a haven from nuclear holocaust. This film was applauded by Catholics for its portrayal of harmonious community life but criticized severely by others for its sentimental, uncritical portrayal of an American scientist and the military superiority and arrogance that America displayed in Spain at the time. As bitterness grew against America as a Franco client, references to America in Spanish cinema became almost nonexistent.

## Plácido (1961)

Berlanga's long-standing artistic collaboration with scriptwriter Rafael Azcona began with *Plácido*. Azcona has helped Berlanga express more acutely the suffering, hyprocrisy, and intolerance that humans inflict upon each other. Berlanga's best films have been written by Azcona, who has heightened Berlanga's awareness of social problems and shares his darkly comic mode of expression.

Plácido González, owner of a three-wheeled motorcycle in a small Spanish town, volunteers his vehicle to distribute fruit baskets for the local Christmas charity drive. But Plácido must pay his note on the cycle, due Christmas Eve, or the vehicle will be repossessed. The conflict between the charity event whose motto is "Cene con un pobre" (Take a beggar to dinner) and Plácido's mortgage payment leads to confusion and disaster, Berlanga's favorite situations. The underlying attitude of the campaign organizers is expressed by such comments as "¿Va usted a recoger a su pobre?" (Are you going to pick up your beggar?) or "¿Qué le ha tocado, anciano del asilo o pobre normal?" (Which did you get, one from the asylum or one from the street?). Such comments reveal the mechanical and essentially repugnant reaction of the bourgeois providers of charity. One of the indigents falls ill and Plácido, desperately trying to reach a notary, agrees to find a doctor. Doña Encarna, the beggar's hostess, is horrified when she discovers that the old man is not married to the woman he has been living with for many years. She insists that a priest be found to marry them and begs Plácido, "Hurry, they are living in sin." The dying beggar refuses to marry, but his wishes are of no importance. The priest pronounces him married to his common-law wife and thus the sensibilities of the bourgeois hostess are respected. Plácido, finally able to pay his note at midnight, goes home to his family. They are waiting until he returns to eat their Christmas dinner, one of the fruit baskets. But on the way home the fruit vendor spies the basket under the motorcycle seat and unjustly accuses Plácido of stealing it. So the tired and hungry family ride home without their Christmas dinner, the banner "Bienvenidos Peregrinos de la Ciudad" (Welcome beggars) still bobbing over the deserted street in the wind. The family's hunger confirms the theme that the rich are not really interested in the poor but rather in charity as a salve to their consciences. The wishes of the poor, from requests for brandy to brace the cold wind to being left to die old and unmarried, are ignored by the more affluent benefactors.

## El verdugo (The Executioner) (1963)

This macabre farce, one of Berlanga's masterpieces, ranks among the best of twentieth-century Spain's works of dramatic art. Like the farces of the theater of the absurd, or the *esperpentos* of Valle-Inclán, *El verdugo* is based on the conflict between personal liberty and responsibility. This simple story, however, is complicated by several important subthemes— submission to social and professional conventions, the executioner as victim, the inescapable corruption of innocence—from which rise a series of comic situations. The laughter produced is an ambiguous expression of both relief and horror at the ultimate, inevitable complicity of the protagonist in a system against which he struggles in vain.

The role of Amadeo, the retiring executioner, becomes totally believable when enacted by the seventy-eight-year-old Pepe Isbert. Known primarily as a comic actor, Isbert creates a delicate balance in this ironic role between the crafty old codger and the clown. Men have always avoided a hangman's woman, but José Luis (Nino Manfredi), a jail guard, falls for Carmen (Emma Penella), Amadeo's attractive daughter. José Luis and Carmen want to marry but have no place to live. As a state official, Amadeo has a guaranteed apartment which he must give up when he retires. He arranges for José Luis to inherit his job so that the couple may have a decent apartment.

The old man is content in his retirement years surrounded by his fam-

Nino Manfredi as José Luis in Luis Berlanga's *El verdugo* (1963).

ily, but José Luis is horrified of becoming an executioner. He refuses until Amadeo assures him that because of legal appeals and delays he will probably not have to carry out his duties. José Luis, who has been living in a cramped, crowded flat with his brother's family, is eager to improve his living standard, so he allows himself to be persuaded.

The social status of the executioner is a rich source for Berlanga's gallows humor. The opening shot is a close-up of a pair of hands crumbling bread into soup: the desk clerk at the jail tries to eat lunch. A coffin passes by containing the latest victim of capital punishment. It is accompanied by Amadeo, who politely wishes the clerk "Buen apetito." The young man pushes his bowl away. Funeral jokes abound throughout the film and provide such gags as a wife's discovery that the man in the coffin at her husband's funeral is not her husband. When the executioners don eighteenth-century costume, complete with wigs and three-cornered hats, and take off on their motorcycle for the garroting of an aristocrat, Berlanga suggests that capital punishment is an outmoded and antique way of dealing with criminals.

Political metaphors lend an undercurrent of protest to *El verdugo*. The old state executioner, undoubtedly intended to be associated with Franco, has come to be considered an endearing benefactor who loves his family and who pulls strings to see that they are well placed. The recipients (that

A coffin arrives at the morgue in Berlanga's *El verdugo* (1963).

is, Spain itself), however, accept his favors unwillingly. The moment of truth for José Luis arrives one day and interrupts a lovemaking session with his wife. He is served with a summons to appear in Palma de Majorca for an execution. Carmen and Amadeo are delighted at the prospect of a vacation. José Luis, too, enjoys himself in Palma when a legal appeal delays the punishment. But his vacation ends abruptly when he is escorted to the jail by Civil Guards. There the unwilling executioner waits for the sentence to be carried out.

Jail guards order champagne for the criminal as his last wish. The criminal changes his mind, however, so the wine is given to the trembling executioner. José Luis still refuses to do his job, but the guards insist. The criminal has confessed and is ready for his fate. Two groups of guards drag the terrified criminal and executioner into a courtyard. Censors cut only one minute from this scene, but it included details which would have helped bring its horror home in spite of the comedy—the face-to-face confrontation between victim and executioner and the sound of the garroting irons.

The final scene is a simple and ironic explanation of the conflict of *El verdugo*. Carmen and her new baby wait on board a tourist ship in the harbor. A car pulls up and Amadeo helps out of it the shaken José Luis. Carmen greets José Luis by asking if he has eaten. She hands him a sandwich, but he is not hungry. "Never again," he mutters. "I'll never do it again." Amadeo pats and consoles him: "I said that too the first time." As the ship pulls away from the dock, dance music plays and passengers wave good-bye. This chilling remark suggests that, like his father and his grand-father, the child in Carmen's arms may one day hear the same words from José Luis as barbarous death dealing is not only tolerated but passes to yet another supposedly civilized generation of Spaniards.

*El verdugo* was not well received by foreign critics, who expected a consistent analogy between the executioner and Franco. Robert Bena-youn blames Berlanga for making a fascist film showing the executioner-dictator to be lovable and kind.[2] But *El verdugo* goes beyond facile anal-ogy with one individual to indict an entire society. The option of a cruel job is offered to José Luis by Amadeo. This option, however, is forced upon him by a web of social and material expectations that have become rigid conventions in most Western societies. José Luis is urged to marry "like normal people" by his brother and family in spite of his own wishes to go to Germany to study mechanics. Thus the protagonist is deprived by the social demands of marriage and family. Moral and economic con-ditions of life in Spain, which give official death dealing professional status, only demean life further so that, from generation to generation, cruelty becomes tolerated, accepted, and, finally, an economically viable way of life.

*El verdugo,* filmed in black and white, is an astounding balance of farce and horror. The viewer never quite becomes accustomed to the sight of coffins leaning on jail walls or comic funerals. Juxtapositions of incon-gruous moods are shot in high contrast, emphasizing shrouds and the menacing shapes of costumes associated with official duties. Yet these jux-tapositions are treated so casually that when Amadeo talks shop with a friend at a picnic about the forms of execution we laugh but also shiver at the ease with which humane adults discuss cruelty and death. Suspense builds throughout the film until José Luis's refusals are seen to be futile and the inevitable exercise of duty occurs. Berlanga disarms his audience with the waving crowds and tourist shots of Carmen and the baby, the ordinary scenes of daily life, before revealing their link to an almost medi-eval form of torture still used in modern Spain. Berlanga, in this remark-able dark comedy, went further than any Spanish director of the day in undermining the *franquista* myths of duty, honor, and patriotism.

### ¡Vivan los novios! (Long Live the Lovers!) (1969)

"Yo me había planteado una especie de ciclo sobre la mujer como de-voradora, que se iniciaba con *La boutique,* seguía con *¡Vivan los novios!* continuaba con *A mi querida mamá en el día de su santo* que nunca se hizo, y terminaba con *Tamaño natural*" (I had planned a kind of series about the devouring woman, which began with *La boutique,* continued with *¡Vivan los novios!* was to include *A mi querida mamá . . .* , which was never made, and ended with *Tamaño natural*) (p. 119). What Hernández Les rightly described as Berlanga's worst film is worth analysis for two reasons—its jumbled, repulsive visual style and its attack on women. Both are characteristic of Berlanga's work. The theme of entrapment, posed in *El verdugo,* is exaggerated in the farcical *¡Vivan los novios!* so that its central character, Leo, is entirely in the power of women.

This caricature of the banker from Burgos who remains a hopeless bumpkin is fully exploited by the comic actor José Luis López Vásquez, who plays Leo as a hopeless clown. Leo, who goes to Sitges for his wedding, is accompanied by his mother. She is a huge, rich, revolting slob whose baggage is labeled "La Burgalesa" (The Lady from Burgos). A visual pun reinforces her image as a piece of luggage when, through her fear of stairs, she has to be lowered from the plane in a baggage bin.

Leo will be married the next day to his fiancée, Loli, who owns a clothing shop. Yet no woman passes him without his ogling her, indicating his lifelong sexual repression. Throughout the first reel, Leo, who stutters a bit around women, chases girls, gets lost in other people's apartments, and is generally sexually deprived and infantile. Leaving his mother floating in a chair in the hotel pool, Leo goes for a night on the town before his wedding the next day. He is about to follow an Irish girl to her hotel when his future brother-in-law grabs him. He goes back to his hotel only to discover that Mamá has fallen from her chair and drowned in the pool.

The macabre juxtaposition of a wedding and a funeral also derives from *El verdugo,* in which funerals become so much a part of daily life that they are often seen as comic. Leo, Loli, and her brother decide not to ruin the wedding with a funeral, but they now have the problem of what to tell the guests about Mamá. They ice down the cadaver in a bathtub and proceed with the wedding preparations. With a body in the bathtub, however, the action becomes ludicrous. The wedding is held, after which the priest, Leo, friends, and relatives pushing baby carriages all march down the street. They are accompanied not by sounds of the traditional wedding recessional but by bullfight music, indicating that Leo is indeed a victim. But of what?

The final sequence of *¡Vivan los novios!* is among Berlanga's best. The day of the funeral begins with a close shot of a black angel—the angel of death. The camera tracks off to reveal the angel as part of the hearse decor. The funeral procession begins slowly, led by Leo, who is followed by the coffin. The funeral is viewed as part of daily life. Tourists, outnumbering the mourners, mingle with the procession while three or four people hand out leaflets, a frequent nuisance on Spanish streets. Leo's mind is not on grief but on the Irish girl whom he recalls in black-and-white inserts that rapidly flick on the screen, showing her kissing his cheek.

Suddenly Leo looks up. High overhead is his object of desire, the Irish girl on a sky-kite, waving. He waves back and begins to run after her, deserting the procession and the coffin. Again he is grabbed by family members who pull him back in line. An overhead shot reveals the procession, with mourners straggling at angles from the hearse, taking on the shape of a huge black spider.

The family unit which in *El verdugo* made a victim of the young protagonist who wanted to study in Germany has become in *¡Vivan los novios!* a black spider whose web entangles Leo. Berlanga sees women as the primary spinners of the family web. As in Spanish drama, which has never dealt seriously with the figure of the mother, Berlanga's Mamá is a helpless buffoon.

The pace of *¡Vivan los novios!* is one of constant motion and confusion from the airport to arrival at Loli's shop where a girl in a bikini tries on a wedding veil. Leo is always on the move, following fresh tracks. He climbs about the hotel roof trying to enter two women's apartments. Male infantilism is underscored when Leo discovers a man lying in bed with a rubber nurser in his mouth attended by two women. Later, this man is seen outside with the nurser hanging on a string from his belt. The farce is at its worst when an angry Loli throws a pie at Leo; he ducks and the pie lands on the cadaver lying in the bathtub.

A frantic pace and bad jokes do not entirely obscure the critical value of *¡Vivan los novios!* Berlanga ridicules very real targets: the rigid family structure, its repressive codes of sexual behavior, its supermom, and its result—a fawning, immature son. As in *El verdugo*, Berlanga also refers to Spaniards' lack of freedom in their own country. Foreigners overrun Sitges and enjoy its pleasures without having to be bound by Spain's repressive morality. The Irish girl, the American boy who bumps into another American on his way out of the Metro, the character in the morgue, Amnésico, who can't remember who he is but speaks English, all represent familiar jokes to Spaniards who, during the *franquista* period, lacked in their own country economic power and social freedoms which foreign visitors enjoyed there.

This often thin farce thus contains some of Berlanga's sharpest social satire. Carlos Heredero points to it as the director's "obra más feista, más despreocupada, menos artificial" (crudest, most careless, least artificial work).[3] Clearly, Berlanga is not here concerned with such niceties as film style, color, or organization. He had admitted that "nunca he cuidado mucho, aunque quizá más al principio de mi carrera, la fotografía" (I have never taken too much care, although perhaps I did at the beginning of my career, with cinematography) (p. 116). As with Buñuel, film style is less important to Berlanga than the communication of ideas. In the unparalleled final sequence of *¡Vivan los novios!* Berlanga equates Spain with a large spider whose future is to conform rigidly to ritual and outworn traditions. This entire frothy film is worth that single, unforgettable image.

### Tamaño natural (Life Size) (1973)

Made in Paris and banned in Spain for two years, *Tamaño natural* is Berlanga's most controversial film. Feminists in Rome condemned it for treating women as objects, a charge Berlanga does not deny: "*Life size* no es un filme antifeminista, a lo sumo sí un filme misógino. Pero . . . para mí, la misoginia es una forma de reconocimiento de la superioridad de la mujer, una forma de aversión a la mujer en cuanto que sentida como superior (*Life size* is not an antifeminist film, at most it is a misogynistic film. But for me misogyny is a form of recognition of the superiority of women, a form of aversion to a superior being).[4] *Tamaño natural,* variously acclaimed as brilliant[5] and condemned as masturbatory,[6] is, along with *El verdugo,* among Berlanga's best. It carries to their logical conclusions his most characteristic preoccupations—freedom versus power and the castrating woman.

Michel, a dentist, orders a life-size polyurethane doll, which arrives in a box stamped "made in Japan." The doll is remarkably lifelike. Michel becomes so entranced with it that he leaves his wife and finally his dental practice to play with it. His wife, Isabelle, is horrified when she discovers that her husband's new love is a doll. In protest one afternoon Isabelle assumes the pose the doll was in when she first saw her—sitting topless in a wheelchair. When Isabelle fails to gain Michel's sympathy (he dumps her in the closet as he does his doll), she stands up and begins pounding him, shouting, "Ella no se pega" (She doesn't fight).

Unlike Isabelle, Henri the divorce lawyer is amused at his friend's imagination. Henri and his wife visit Michel on his birthday and bring him as a present a doll of traditional size and clothing. Michel, not a bit embarrassed, goes along with the joke, "pero podías ahorrarte la molestia . . . ya tenemos una niña" (but you could save yourself the trouble . . . we already have a child).[7] He tiptoes to the bedroom to show his incredulous friends his child, who lies content at the doll's breast. By closing the camera in on the unexpected view of a doll cradling a child, Berlanga raises one of the film's more intriguing questions: can the child's beneficial relationship with a doll be in any way extended into adulthood?

Michel (Michel Piccoli) weds a doll in Luis Berlanga's *Tamaño natural* (1973).

Berlanga seems to inquire if substitution of plastic surrogates for release of, for example, sexual aggression might represent a specific social
benefit. For Michel's doll, pampered and cuddled by her owner, is also the
object of outrageous angry displays triggered by the same feelings of jealousy, lust, and betrayal that men feel toward women. After the porter,
who comes to Michel's room to fix the radiator, rapes the doll, Michel,
who has videotaped the porter's orgy, attempts to knife his plastic partner. The only blood, however, is shed by Michel, an ominous clue to *Tamaño natural*'s final outcome.

Berlanga has called *Tamaño natural* "un discurso sobre la soledad" (a
discourse on solitude), a theme which accounts for the film's underlying
bitterness (pp. 180–181). For Michel, isolated and enjoying sensual pleasures with a model of the perfect woman, finds that he is still subject to
conventional emotions toward women. Berlanga concludes, "Ni siquiera
una mujer perfecta puede ayudar a un hombre" (Not even a perfect
woman can help a man) (p. 181). This is a valuable social lesson, especially for feminists who rage against *Tamaño natural*. Once it is understood that woman-as-object offers no final satisfaction to male desire,
women themselves are liberated from the need to resemble or to act as
objects. *Tamaño natural* leads males and females through a maze of sex-

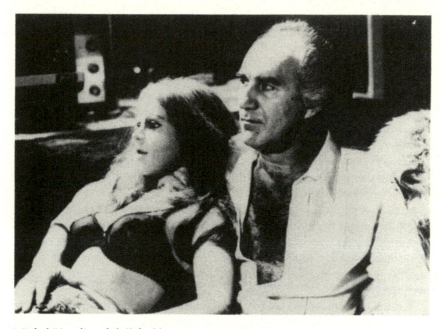

Michel Piccoli and doll find happiness in Berlanga's *Tamaño natural* (1973).

ual behavior only to discover the existential anguish that lies at the core of
the human condition. As Diego Galán points out, *Tamaño natural* is
Berlanga's most pessimistic film, for it reveals that total personal freedom
leads to disaster.[8]

Michel is ultimately defeated, not, of course, by the doll but by his own
reactions to it. During a visit by some Spanish émigrés who come to his
apartment to cheer him when he has a cold, the doll is stolen. Michel
tracks the Spaniards to their *barrio* where they, typically, set the doll up as
the Holy Virgin in a mock religious procession. The procession, led by a
man on his knees with the doll as a holy relic in the background, is a
hilarious reference to national sexual mores, in which Spanish males see
women as either virgins or whores. Michel arrives in time to see the doll
fall from its pedestal into a group of male Spaniards, who attack the doll
sexually from all angles.

Michel rescues the doll and drives with it about the deserted Paris
streets at dawn. Feeling betrayed and disillusioned, he carries on a monologue with his plastic partner: "¡Qué crees, que voy a llevarte a casa, que
te voy a perdonar? Sería absurdo, nadie lleva a su casa un cadaver . . . yo
estoy también muerto" (Do you think I'm going to take you home? That
I'm going to pardon you? It would be absurd, nobody takes a cadaver

home . . . I, too, am dead) (p. 136). Suddenly he swerves and drives off into the Seine. A medium shot observes the car and driver sink, and they are seen no more. But the doll rises to the surface and bobs about in the murky water as an astonished man watches from the bridge. The film ends with a long shot of this observer staring at the doll, a shot which hints that the entire action could be replayed with any male protagonist. This closure was improvised when Berlanga noticed a bystander watching the scene being filmed. It signals an underlying fear that the male will be swallowed up while the indestructible female only bounces back for more.

*Tamaño natural* is an amusing but disturbing play upon the doll/ woman-as-object motif. The motif is not new to Spanish theater; it was used by Jacinto Grau in one of his best plays, *El señor del Pigmalión* (1921). Pigmalion, a puppeteer, falls in love with one of his puppets but is killed by one of them when they rebel against him. Berlanga updates the theme with erotic jokes and timely reference to questions of male-female relationships at a moment in which these questions are part of a larger inquiry into the durability of traditional marriage in a contemporary world.

For the first time in his career, Berlanga focuses upon the personality of a protagonist isolated from a social context. Actor Michel Piccoli performs this demanding solo role with admirable control and off-handed ease. Berlanga's camera moves in closer to its subject than usual but still favors medium and long shots to grasp the doll's appearance in its surroundings and the reactions of others to it. Visual surprise is repeated when an unidentified woman, dressed in Victorian costume, is seen from behind talking to Michel's eighty-year-old mother. The joke is on the viewer and Michel when we discover that his mother, who lacks companionship, has dressed the doll as a friend and sits chatting with her in her dressing room.

While the doll is frequently nude and is the object of violent sexual assault, *Tamaño natural* is neither erotic nor pornographic. It is more along the lines of Buñuel's *Archibaldo de la Cruz*, a study of sexual aggression. Like Archi, whose desire to kill women is pathological, triggered by the recall of a childhood incident, Michel is seen as an entirely normal male. He, too, however, acts in an infantile way in his relations with women, preferring his fantasy to the real world, his plastic woman to real women . *Tamaño natural* is a remarkable sexual morality tale in which the protagonist, in complete freedom, plays at sex without gaining any lasting enjoyment.

Populist, spontaneous, anarchic, the films of Berlanga are as authentic an expression of the Spanish character in the twentieth century as Lope de Vega's plays were in the seventeenth. Indeed, Berlanga might have been the Lope of Spanish cinema had not censorship distorted his career. In spite of censorship, however, Berlanga's films have enriched his country's dramatic tradition. If Tirso de Molina created the character of don Juan on the Spanish stage in the seventeenth century, Berlanga in Spanish film updates and discovers new dimensions to this universal type.

# 6. Late Postwar Years: 1960–1975

Official interest in a strong national film industry is not apparent in Spain until 1962, when the country made its first effort to enter the European Common Market. In a concerted effort to demonstrate that Spain at least culturally was no longer the retrograde, fascist backwater of Europe, a new era of *aperturismo* was instigated. Incoming minister of information and tourism Manuel Fraga Iribarne brought back as director of the Departamento de Cinematografía y Teatro the moderate García Escudero, dismissed a decade earlier for defending *Surcos*. García Escudero had participated in the Salamanca talks and knew well the frustrations and complaints of those trying to make films in Franco's Spain. So, when the tides of censorship temporarily receded in 1962, García Escudero began to excavate the agenda of the Salamanca talks which, like a shipwreck on the ocean floor, had remained undisturbed for seven long years.

Among the first improvements in the national climate of film culture was the opening of the Filmoteca, Spain's official film archives. Established almost a decade earlier, in 1953, the Filmoteca had been inactive until May 1963, when it began public screenings. Under the direction of Franco loyalist Carlos Fernández Cuenca, the Filmoteca had always been last on the regime's list of priorities. It had been relegated since its inception to two offices in a building occupied by No-Do. Funds for film purchase, restoration of prints, or even storage of its two hundred feature films and approximately one hundred Civil War documentaries were not provided. In the estimate of recent former director Floriano Soria, 90 percent of Spain's film history has been lost due to disregard for preservation.[1] The primary activity of the Filmoteca during its first decade was the publication of film monographs by the *franquista* film historian Fernández Cuenca. It also served an educational function by helping to familiarize the public, especially film students, with film. The Filmoteca was long awaited and well received. After five years of operation, however, it fell victim to the closing down of *apertura*. Public screenings ceased in 1967, not to resume until 1972.

Updating the censorship code was García Escudero's next and most difficult task. Attacked by progressive critics as a tool of the establishment and by the right wing and the church as a promoter of *anormalidades repulsivas* (repulsive abnormalities),[2] García Escudero began to see Madrid as a kind of Siberia and himself as Muñoz Fontán, victim of *l'affaire Viridiana*.[3] Having put forth revised codes in February 1963, he saw them subjected to almost immediate attacks aimed at reinstating more stringent measures (Reglamiento de la Rama de Censura de Clasificación y Censura, 1964). When it appeared that many of the young new film directors were voices of opposition, censorship rose to silence their protest, so that the new voices were, for the most part, muffled.

García Escudero was unable to marshal sufficient political support to seriously alter censorship, but he was able to establish, in 1962, a category for noncommercial, artistically valuable *cine de interés especial,* or special interest films. This category made it possible for young directors fresh from IIEC, renamed the Escuela Oficial de Cinematografía (EOC), to make films in an industry that had always excluded young professionals except as apprentices. In opposition to the genres of *cine oficial* (the tired war films, historical epics, and folklore musicals), the special interest category created a new genre in Spanish film. Realistic narratives dealing with contemporary settings and current problems, often critical of Spanish society, this new genre became known by critic Juan Francisco de Lasa's term as the *nuevo cine español,* or New Spanish Cinema.

The New Spanish Cinema derives, in its use of metaphor to deliver social criticism, from the Bardem and Berlanga films of the 1950s. In their preoccupation with Spain and its problems, however, the New Spanish directors drew upon the literary Generation of 1898. Just as Unamuno, Baroja, and Antonio Machado searched for answers to Spain's current dilemmas in its historical, literary, even geographical past, the young filmmakers of the 1960s analyzed and often satirized Spain's social traditions in an effort to create a visual image of their country in which Spain might see itself for what it is, rather than what it had been or hoped it might be. Some of the New Spanish films were mediocre, including Basilio Martín Patino's *Nueve cartas a Berta* (1965), Manuel Summers's *Juguetes rotos* (1966), and Mario Camus's *Con el viento solano* (1965). Others, including Miguel Picazo's *La tía Tula* (1964), Angelino Fons's *La busca* (1966), and Carlos Saura's *La caza* (1966), are among Spain's best and are discussed in Chapter 9 in detail.

In spite of the special censorship status accorded the New Spanish films as works of special interest, young Spanish directors were still harassed by censorship. Four minutes were cut from Picazo's *La tía Tula,* and footage in Saura's *Llanto por un bandido,* featuring Buñuel as an executioner, was not only cut but confiscated and destroyed by censors. Manuel Summers recalls his own careful autocensorship in preparation of the script of *Juguetes rotos*. Yet Summers received censors' reply of "pues, no" and a list of prohibited shots, including those of a child begging, girls in bikinis, and a piece of dialogue saying "Cualquier español puede ser torero" (Any Spaniard can be a bullfighter). These continued restrictions discouraged many promising directors, such as Picazo, who made only one more film before he abandoned cinema for television.

Among those most instrumental in creating the New Cinema was not a director but a producer, Elías Querejeta. A former soccer player turned scriptwriter and film director, Querejeta produced ten films by New Spanish Cinema directors in the decade of the 1960s and eight in the 1970s. In fact, some of Spain's finest films have been produced by Querejeta, including Saura's *La prima Angélica* (1973), Ricardo Franco's *Pascual Duarte* (1976), and Victor Erice's *El espíritu de la colmena* (1973).

From the government's point of view, the New Spanish Cinema was a showcase operation in which films for consumption outside Spain were produced. It was Querejeta who was able to package the violence and distortions of the Spanish experience in a style both visually interesting to a foreign audience and, more importantly, permissible by the Franco regime. There were several reasons for Querejeta's success. He was able to gather and work consistently with one of the best technical crews in the country, consisting of assistant director José Luis Ruiz Marcos, cinematographer Luis Cuadrado, composer Luis de Pablo, production manager Primitivo Alvaro, and cameraman Teodoro Escamilla, who skillfully articulated what has come to be known as *la estética de la represión* (the aesthetic of repression),[4] characteristic of the highly metaphorical style of Spanish films critical of Franco and of the Spanish bourgeoisie responsible for retaining the dictator in power for forty-three years.

Since the New Spanish Cinema turned out to be a voice of opposition, the government devised a way to control distribution of these films so that they were seen in Spain by the tiniest audiences possible. A system of art theaters was devised, along the lines of the *théâtres d'art et d'essai* in Paris, enabling foreign films to be screened in their original versions. New Spanish Cinema could be seen almost exclusively in these by a small, discriminating, educated audience.

The *arte y ensayo* system began in January 1967, with 380 theaters which could not, by law, seat over 500 and which were permissible only in urban areas—cities of over 500,000 inhabitants. At first, distributors were delighted to be able to offer films screened in Spain for the first time—Polanski's *Repulsion*, Truffaut's *Jules et Jim*, Resnais's *Hiroshima, mon amour*, Godard's *A bout de souffle*. But crowds were small. To boost box-office sales, exhibitors displayed lurid advertisements, promising the public it could see at the *arte y ensayo* theaters *fruto prohibido* (films censored elsewhere). While this was true, the mass public came looking for salacious material. It was disappointed to find that most previously censored films were not necessarily sexually explicit, such as Antonioni's *L'Avventura,* Buñuel's *Exterminating Angel,* Bresson's *Le Journal d'un curé de campagne,* and Bergman's *Persona.*

A disillusioned public, entirely unprepared through years of censorship for new developments in film, stopped patronizing art theaters in Spain, so exhibitors began to revert to commercial programming. By 1972 the art theater was discontinued, having proved to be an unsuccessful experiment. One of the hidden keys to the short lifespan of the *teatro de arte y ensayo* lies in the law that created it. Written in 1969, the law, buried in an Orden Ministerial de Información y Turismo, proposes art theater permits because of "el desbordamiento creciente en los últimos años de la población turística, que por razones idiomáticas difícilmente puede asistir a espectáculos cinematográficos en nuestro pais" (the growing flood of tourists in recent years which for reasons of language is not easily able to attend movies in our country).[5]

This remarkable statement reveals the thinking behind not only the art theaters in Spain but also the New Spanish Cinema which was exhibited in them. These special theaters were created not so much for the benefit of the Spanish film industry but so that foreign tourists in Spain could see movies in their native language. Spanish films of special interest (that is, the New Spanish Cinema) were exhibited almost exclusively in the art theaters. When, after only five years, these were abolished, Spain's own New Cinema was without a public in its own country.

The closing of the *teatro de arte y ensayo* signaled the death of the New Spanish Cinema. The movement had been beset with problems from its inception due to the enormous lack of film culture in Spain, where almost no film—foreign or domestic—was shown in its original version when first released. Works by the New Spanish Cinema directors already seemed dated to foreign audiences.[6] When, for example, García Escudero sent Patino's *Nueve cartas a Berta* to Cannes, it was rejected as being of no interest to an international public, whose national problems and understanding of cinema had advanced considerably beyond those of Patino's honest but naive film.[7]

A fair assessment of the New Spanish Cinema must acknowledge the accomplishment of García Escudero, its promoter and confessor, who was justifiably proud of its record. Within the four years from 1962 to 1966, forty-one new directors had made their first film. A temporary scratch in the granite face of censorship was carved by the art theater and special interest films category. As the director general stated in an interview, "En 1962 abrimos las puertas de la profesión . . . y ninguna 'ola nueva' llega a los 10 años" (In 1962 we opened the doors of the profession . . . and no "new wave" lasts ten years).[8]

García Escudero occupied an almost impossible position. Like a Catholic father, he warned Spaniards against expecting censorship to save them from evil movies: "El ejercicio de la censura . . . se debe sujetar a un . . . respeto máximo de la libertad ajena" (The exercise of censorship . . . should be subject to . . . a maximum respect for general freedom).[9] Under constant siege from both right and left, he must have developed a slight schizophrenia, for while he worked to create a genre of religious film he found that Pasolini's *Evangelio según San Mateo* (*Book of St. Matthew*) "tiene una vibración auténticamente religiosa . . . aunque . . . los realizadores de *El evangelio según San Mateo* y de *La Biblia* no sean ni siquiera creyentes" (has a genuinely religious tone . . . although . . . the directors of the *Book of St. Matthew* and of *The Bible* may not even be believers).[10]

The *primera apertura* gave rise to a subgenre of films even less commercially viable than the New Spanish Cinema. This subgenre consists of avant-garde fantasy and horror pieces by a group of filmmakers to whom critic Ricardo Muñoz Suay referred in Catalán with the name Escola de Barcelona, the Barcelona School, Spain's most progressive alternative to the New Spanish Cinema. Among the directors of this genre were Vicente Aranda, who returned from Venezuela to his native Barcelona and began, with critic Román Gubern, making films. The two collaborated on *Brillante porvenir* (1964). Aranda then set out in his own direction with a horror thriller, *Fata Morgana* (1965), based on a story by Gonzálo Suárez.

Suárez, one of the best prose writers of the postwar era as well as a successful sports columnist, wrote under the pseudonym Martin Gerard. Suárez's sportswriting was so lucrative that he was able to finance his experiments with cinema. The first of these was *Ditirambo* (1967), a rather inept manipulation of a shy and fearful hero caught in a fantasy of terror. Suárez's years of experimentation concluded in 1974, when he directed the commercially successful, masterly adaptation of Clarín's nineteenth-century novel *La regenta* (*The Judge's Wife*), starring two of Spain's best film actors, Fernando Rey and Ana Belén.

Before the Civil War, Barcelona had been the center of film activity in Spain. The four large studios located there constituted the country's film capital. So advanced were these studios that most of the Civil War documentaries were made by Catalán filmmakers, mostly Republicans, who had either worked or trained in Barcelona. Franco's victory obliterated this activity so completely that postwar film in Spain was, until the 1960s, centered entirely in Madrid under the obsessively watchful eye of the regime.

With the first opportunity offered by *apertura*, the Barcelona School, like a rare plant growing through hairline cracks in the fascist façade, began to appear. Unconcerned with attracting a public and ignoring the *franquista* myths, Barcelona directors tried to differentiate themselves from their more sober, socially aware colleagues in Madrid. They concentrated instead on fantasy, a genre which allowed them to play with cinema techniques. They distinguished themselves by forging the only avant-garde cinema in the country as well as engaging in the only film activity truly independent of Madrid. At the same time they had no choice but to remain marginal in postwar cinema. As critics Marta Hernández and Manuel Revuelta remark dryly, their only public were the censors because even the fringe was subject to state surveillance.[11]

One of the Barcelona directors, Jacinto Esteva Grewe, set up his own studio, Films-contacto, in which he produced his dadaist *Dante no es únicamente severo* (1967) and *Después del deluvio* (1968), as well as *Cada vez que . . . me enamora creo que es para siempre* (1967), by Carlos Durán. This film, reportedly based on a remark Brigitte Bardot is said to have uttered, reveals Durán's training in Paris through slick and glossy images of Barcelona nightlife. Esteva's collaborator on *Dante,* Joaquín Jordá, summed up the predicament of film experimentation in Spain when he confessed, "Como no podemos hacer Victor Hugo, hacemos Mallarmé" (Since we can't do Victor Hugo, we'll do Mallarmé), a remark that reflects the limitations of independence in a fascist dictatorship.[12]

That the Barcelona School not only existed but was able to participate sporadically in mainstream cinema is proof of its talent and ingenuity in opposition to monolithic government control. Barcelona had always had an active group of amateur filmmakers, and the Barcelona School adopted amateur strategies hoping to avoid the restraints endemic to the Spanish film industry. By using nonprofessional actors, directors, and distributors and by working in teams of individuals, all of whom shared in the various phases of film production, they were able to achieve a degree of independence unknown to filmmakers in Madrid.

If the School of Barcelona was unable to influence major film genres, it achieved its impact upon Spanish film indirectly, through an intense lobbying group called the Sitgistas. When García Escudero was replaced for the second time as director general of Cinematografía y Teatro, there were two reasons for his dismissal. One was economic; the other, unstated, resulted from his inability to control restless voices of dissent on the fringe. This fringe (students and young directors), presided over by film critic Ramón Gubern, gathered in Sitges, a resort village in Catalonia, only a month before García Escudero's removal. From October 1–6, 1967, they convened the only public discussion of film at a national level held in twelve years, the Primeras Jornadas Internacionales de Escuelas de Cinematografía (First International Film Schools' Discussions), planned and attended primarily by film students.

The Sitges conference was a product of the extraordinary energy of the Barcelona School. Its theorist, Joaquin Jordá, was one of the participants in the conference, along with Antonio Drove, Antonio Artero, Manuel Revuelta, and José Luis García Sánchez. Jordá had announced at the Pesaro (Italy) Film Festival that "today it is not possible to speak freely of reality in Spain, so we're trying to describe its imaginary life." [13] That he spoke in French underlines the strong sense of nationalism felt by the Barcelona filmmakers and their efforts to distinguish themselves as separate and distinct from Madrid and the New Spanish Cinema.

While Jordá used French to distance himself and his group from Madrid, he resorted to Marxist terminology to draft a manifesto that in tone as well as content could not be further from the New Spanish Cinema. The manifesto demanded an end to censorship and state subsidies of any kind that might also serve as an instrument of control. Further, it called for the replacement of the Sindicato Nacional de Espectáculo (State Entertainment Union) with a democratic union that would supervise means of production, distribution, and exhibition. This demand opposed the New Spanish Cinema, which was created as the special category of *cine de interés* and which depended on financial protection to survive in the commercial market.

The Sitges manifesto denounced any effort to make films within the established industry, with or without state subsidy, as collaboration with a corrupt system. While the New Spanish directors welcomed *apertura* as an opportunity to protest the fascist dictatorship by infiltrating their ideas into cinema, the *sitgistas* rejected what they called *posibilismo,* or working within the system, as perpetuation of corruption. They would only tolerate an industry independent of the state or an established industry not beholden to it.

Both the rhetoric and the philosophy of the Sitges manifesto were transparently Marxist. It deplored cinema and art in general as products and tools of the ruling class. This of course was true in postwar Spain, where Franco controlled every form of art. Yet, in denouncing as collaborators those who protested against official culture without proposing a form of revolutionary cinema, the Sitges manifesto remained only a negative force. Ironically, the horror/terror/fantasy genre most characteristic of the Barcelona group was even more evasive of reality than the New Spanish Cinema.

By the time the Franco regime realized the heresies going on at Sitges, the conference was almost over. Nevertheless, the Civil Guards managed to close down some of the sessions and make a few arrests. The group quickly dispersed; Jordá, who eventually abandoned cinema, sought refuge in Rome, and his collaborator's studio, Films-contacto, closed. Film students were punished by the closing of both the Filmoteca, which ceased public screenings for five years, and by the suspension of studies at the National Film School (EOC). Finally, García Escudero's vision of himself as Muñoz Fontán, victim of *l'affaire Viridiana,* was realized: his position as director general was dissolved in November 1967. The Sitges conference, the first public dialogue with the ideological left in postwar Spain, was significant primarily as an indication that *apertura,* the "crack," had sealed tight again and that discussion of independence from or opposition to Franco's cultural policies would still, almost thirty years after the Civil War, not be tolerated.

While the Sitges conference was, for the most part, a gathering of students, critics, and other young professional hopefuls, the problems they discussed—censorship, prior submission of scripts, distribution and exhibition, copros—continued to be those of the Spanish film industry at large. In view of the government's reaction to the Sitges conference, the Spanish film directors' union—Agrupacion Sindical de Directores-Realizadores Españoles de Cinematografía (ASDREC)—was determined that discussion of these problems should proceed, if not in the Marxist rhetoric of leftist students, at least at a professional level of the industry. They planned to continue debate of these issues at their own convention, scheduled to take place November 23, 1969. These professional directors, on the basis of a study they carried out of the problems of Spanish film, proposed to publish the industry's demands. Some of these, including abolishment of censorship, had been made at Sitges; others, such as the inclusion of film professionals on censorship boards, dated as far back as the Salamanca talks of 1955.

The ASDREC convention was prohibited because of the controversial nature of the agenda, but ASDREC persisted. After numerous directors requested a special session to discuss the topics most vital to the industry, the meeting was held in March 1970. Predictably, their recommendations echoed those of Salamanca and Sitges in calling for an end to censorship and inclusion of industry professionals on censorship boards.

To the clamor of students and directors for the abolishment of censorship, producers added their outcry. By March 1970 the government owed them three hundred million pesetas in back payment for subsidies.[14] These subsidies came from fees for dubbing foreign films for TV and cinema and subtitling permits, and many of them were never collected.[15] As

Spanish film confronted its crises of the early 1970s its quality declined. The best achievement of the past decade, the New Spanish Cinema, never gained commercial status because it was never released to the mass public in its country of origin. It was allowed by the state to perform as planned— as a brilliant but brief signal to Europe that Spain, under special circumstances, could produce first-rate cinema.

With the demise of García Escudero and the New Spanish Cinema and the dissolution of the School of Barcelona and its vanguardist fringe, movie screens in Spain were dominated by the popular genres of the decade—spy movies in endless repetition of James Bond with their terror, violence, and mild eroticism, and spaghetti, or *chorizo* (sausage), Westerns, as they were known in Spain (*chorizo,* like spaghetti, being a cheap, widely consumed product of individual strings indistinguishable one from another). Of dismal artistic value, the chorizos were enormously popular and occasionally attracted young directors who could not find work elsewhere, such as José Luis Borau, who bolstered his sagging career with *Brandy* (1963).

Most of the Spanish Westerns were coproductions with Italy or Hollywood. They starred actors in professional decline in their own countries (Lee Van Cleef, Edmund Purdom) or Spanish actors who assumed American pseudonyms. This practice was a bitter comment on the genre, since it was both a way to disguise having worked in Westerns as well as a way to make them seem as purely American, and thus as authentic, as possible.

Often made with interchangeable sets, without scripts, and in groups of two or three at a time, the Spanish Western rapidly began to decline. Christian values of defense of the weak and the pursuit of justice, characteristic of the early American Westerns, were inverted.[16] There developed comic Westerns, paralleling *True Grit* and *Butch Cassidy and the Sundance Kid,* in which crimes had no motive beyond the enjoyment of violence for its own sake. These comic chorizos, such as *Y le llamaban halcón* (*And They Called Him Falcon*) (1971), mocked the rhetoric of sacrifice of the official *cine cruzada,* the fascist war films of prior decades. In *Para mí el oro . . . para tí el plomo* (*Gold for Me, Lead for You*), a band of marauders dress in priest's garb, call themselves the Band of Priests, and utter expressions such as "Santo colt" (Holy Colt).[17] This kind of western, including *Reverendo Colt* and *Un colt por cuatro cirios* (*Four Candles for a Colt*), both of 1971, and *Tedeum* (1972), was, like the picaresque novel which originated in Spain in the sixteenth century, almost a protest genre. The outcast underdog of the comic Western, like Quevedo's socially marginal *pícaro,* mirrors the crudity and violence of the society around him but stops short of posing serious remedies or solutions.

Perhaps one of the reasons for the overwhelming and long-lived popularity of this genre was its easy translatability into images identified with Spanish culture. The Indian roles opposing the cowboys were often played by laborers or gypsies who lived in areas where exterior panoramic shots were being made and who would work for minimal wages. Because of the Mediterranean facial characteristics of these individuals, it seemed natural to set the action of the film in revolutionary Mexico, where conflicts with the United States or with opposing revolutionary factions were plentiful. Titles such as *Gringo* (1963), *Mestizo* and *Adiós gringo* (both of 1965), *Los siete de Pancho Villa* (1966), and *Tequila* (1970), were especially appealing to Spaniards whose sense of historical kinship with Mexico was based on three centuries of colonial rule.

By 1973, when the cowboy and spy thrillers had repeated themselves almost into oblivion, there arose a hybrid genre generally classified as the *tercera vía* (third way) and produced by José Dibildos. Neither fantasies nor films of social criticism, they represented a third way to undercut censorship and yet still remain visible on public screens.

The genre of the *tercera vía* derived from the popular *zarzuelas,* or light musical comedies of the turn of the century, and from Italian and American film farces. They were not musicals but comedies whose popular language and situations made them accessible to a mass public, as the more intellectual New Spanish Cinema had never been. Low-brow jokes, often about sex, and deliberate appeal to unsophisticated minds drew criticism from many who knew Spanish directors were capable of quality films. The only redeeming characteristic of the *tercera vía* films was that their jokes contained a grain of social commentary. By touching upon problems which heretofore could not be discussed in Spanish film (abortion, prostitution, birth control, sex before and outside of marriage), they satirized modern life in Spain. Thus they occupied a level above pure commercial genres, such as the violent spaghetti Westerns and spy thrillers, but closer to film farce than to the New Spanish Cinema.

Manuel Summers began working in this mostly frivolous but often thought-provoking genre in the 1960s when he laughed at Spanish attitudes toward birth control in *No somos de piedra* (*We're Only Human*) (1967) and *¿Porqué te engaña tu marido?* (*Why is Your Husband Unfaithful?*) (1968). The genre became firmly established with Roberto Bodegas's *Españolas en París* (*Spanish Girls in Paris*) (1973) and *Vida conyugal sana* (*Healthy Married Life*) (1974), and Antonio Drove's *Tocata y fuga de Lolita* (*Lolita's Tocata and Fugue*) (1974). Characteristic of these harmless, naive, and superficial products is Vicente Escriva's *Lo verde comienza en los Pirineos* (*Sex Starts at the Pyrenees*) (1973) about four typical young men—Manolo, Serafín, Ramón, and Pepe—who go to Biarritz for a fling and to see porno movies. Their wives, furious at being left behind, put on their miniskirts and follow their husbands' example by going to Biarritz for a fling of their own. Inevitably, they encounter their husbands, who are shocked and furious at their wives' daring to do the very things they themselves have enjoyed. After initial fights and threats of divorce, they all return to Spain (where, as Bardem reminded us in 1965, "Nothing Ever Happens") and resume their routine lives. Only Serafín, who is single and lives with his aunt (recall the couple of Marco Ferreri's *El pisito* [1958]), falls in love with a girl, Paula, whom he meets in Biarritz. He marries Paula and thus the film reflects both traditional and modern points of view: the "naughty" escapade has a reassuring outcome—marriage.

The *tercera vía* genre reaches its highest achievement with *El amor del capitán Brando* (1974), directed by Jaime de Armiñán and starring Ana Belén and veteran actor and director Fernando Fernán Gómez. Aurora (Ana Belén) is a village schoolteacher who is fired for her insistence on including sex education as part of the curriculum for sixth-graders. Two men fall in love with this warm and healthy young woman—Fernando, recently returned after decades of exile and still not at home in his homeland, and Juan, one of her students, age thirteen. Castille's landscape, filmed through the lens of the gifted cinematographer Luis Cuadrado, is a key to its character—harsh and unchanging. The boy, who plays at being Captain Brando of the 7th Cavalry, falls for the only loving woman he knows, since his conniving mother tries to convince her son that his French father is dead. Juan is a twentieth-century boy–Don Quixote—confused, isolated, but already capable of passion. His future, as this film, the best of the *tercera vía*, suggests, will not be easy.

The decade of Franco's death opened upon an abyss in Spanish film. The industry was hopelessly in debt, the best of its new genres—the New Spanish Cinema and the experiments of the Barcelona School—were barely visible in their own country. The art theaters, which had been confined to certain demographic and economic requirements (their tickets cost more than those at other movie houses), were closed. The only area of modern life deemed by censors as safe for Spanish viewers from the 1960s until Franco's death was, ironically, that of the human torso, since more and more of it was allowed to be seen in the subporno farces of the *tercera vía* films. What were not relaxed were restrictions upon social criticism and political dissent. As for foreign films, Roger Mortimore was correct when he lamented that the Spanish film public remained "voyeurs," for, if 20 percent of world cinema had been banned in Spain since the Civil War, this percentage increased in the 1970s to 50 percent of films made abroad which could not be seen on Spanish screens.[18]

If world cinema could not be seen in Spain, at least it could be shot there. The brightest event for Spanish film during the decade of the 1960s was the return of Buñuel who, in 1969, had finally been given permission to film *Tristana* in Spain. Buñuel's return was another signal to the world that, while Franco's postwar regime could not tolerate challenge to its myths, it would risk embarrassment again from a director it clearly could never control—Luis Buñuel.

# 7. Luis Buñuel and His Influence

Although he made only two films in postwar Spain, Luis Buñuel had an enormous impact on the Spanish film industry, on the Franco government, and on individual Spanish directors. As a young surrealist whose first three films were banned, Buñuel gained early firsthand insight into the minds of censors. In the immediate prewar years, Buñuel, working anonymously in the Spanish film industry, was able to set high standards and attract talent. When the world-famous director returned to film in his country after years of absence, he had become a legend in Spain.

Buñuel made his first film there in 1932 when his friend Ramón Acín won a lottery ticket and returned the prize money, which Buñuel had loaned him. The film, *Las Hurdes (Tierra sin pan)* (*Las Hurdes [Land without Bread]*) deals with Las Hurdes, a geographically isolated region in Spain. This harsh, rocky region is not far from such centers of culture as Salamanca but remote from economic or cultural improvements. In 1932, its inhabitants were so poor that some had never seen bread. Most *hurdanos* left the region to earn their living and never returned.

With a crew of four, Buñuel spent a month shooting footage of the deprivation, isolation, and poverty of an area that has been called Spain's Appalachia. Lack of basic health care is revealed in searing portraits of a woman with a goiter and emaciated children suffering from mental and physical disease. Lives of abject misery, the film suggests, are ignored by a somnolent church. Children's education stressed not cooperation but the respect of private property, a cruel irony where ownership, even of bread, was unknown. In an ironic comment, Buñuel accompanies scenes of hopelessness and hunger with a sound track of Brahms's Fourth Symphony, underscoring the inability of even the most sublime cultural achievements to improve the lives of people long neglected by a complacent government.

*Las Hurdes* was screened by a small group of upper-class bourgeois and intellectuals, among them Gregorio Marañón. Dr. Marañón, well known for his psychological study of the Don Juan character and numerous essays on a wide range of topics, was also president of a group called the Patronato de Las Hurdes. He objected vigorously to the film. Why, he is reported to have asked Buñuel, did the film include so many images of terrible poverty when he himself had seen carts full of grain being transported there? Buñuel recalls, "Pregunté a Marañón si había visitado Las Hurdes Altas donde la gente no había comido pan. Y aquí finalizó el diálogo" (I asked Marañón if he had visited upper Las Hurdes where the people had not eaten bread. And here the conversation ended).[1]

Three years later, in 1935, a friend of Buñuel's, Ricardo Urgoite, needed a director for his film company, Filmófono. It had been Urgoite who loaned the only copy in Spain of *L'Age d'or* to the Film Club of Buñuel's alma mater, the Residencia de Estudiantes, for its screening by university students. So Buñuel agreed to return to Madrid and work at Filmófono on the provision that his contribution remain anonymous. Filmófono was, after all, a business venture, which Buñuel's surrealist friends in Paris would frown upon.

Buñuel's presence at Filmófono attracted promising and talented people to the studio and could have provided a quality foundation for a Spanish film industry. Four films were made with Buñuel's collaboration. All were of a minimal artistic level but one, *¿Quién me quiere a mí? (Who Loves Me?)*, which Buñuel helped José Luis Sáenz de Heredia direct. It was, when released in 1936, still one of the few Spanish films about divorce.

With the approach of the Civil War, Buñuel left Spain, not to return until Bardem and Uninci took advantage of the 1960 *apertura* to invite him back. The film he made there (*Viridiana*), the scandal it caused, and ensuing political embarrassment to Spain have already been described in the foregoing chapters. Buñuel was persona non grata in Spain until 1969, when he was finally given permission to film *Tristana* (1970) in Toledo and Madrid.

*Tristana,* one of Buñuel's finest, is a good example of why his films, although banned and thus not well known in Spain, were considered by Spanish directors who knew of them as a national treasure. Like all of his Hispanic works, *Tristana* reflects inimitable and profound understanding of Spanish culture and character. The use of Spanish proverbs ("La mujer honrada, pie quebrada y en casa" [To keep a woman honest, break her leg and keep her at home]); scenes of the *tertulias* (groups, mostly of men, gathering in cafés to talk over the issues of the day); use of interiors of Spanish cathedrals with their ornate sarcophagi are all immediately recognizable to almost any Spaniard. The narrow, winding streets of Toledo were among Buñuel's favorite haunts as a university student. Views of these streets at different moments of day and night can be observed in *Tristana.*

The novel on which *Tristana* is based is by Spain's greatest nineteenth-century realist, Benito Pérez Galdós. As in most copros, the female lead role went to a foreign actress, Catherine Deneuve. However French she may be, she plays the role of the orphaned Tristana splendidly. The rest of the cast is Spanish and stars Spain's best—Lola Gaos as the faithful Saturna and Fernando Rey as the aging macho anarchist Don Lope. If Galdós knew these characters during his lifetime and recreated them in what has always been regarded as a second-rate novel, they never came to life until Buñuel filmed them.

As was his practice when adapting novels for the screen (*Nazarin, Belle de jour, The Young One, Diary of a Chambermaid*), Buñuel placed on them the stamp of his own convictions. While *Tristana* is faithful in the portrayal of customs and character, the ending, the era, and innumerable details of action and human relationships are changed by Buñuel for his own purposes. This habit of using novels as a point of departure rather than an end in themselves always infuriated those who preferred the novels. But for young Spanish directors in search of methods to insinuate rather than to state openly, to imply, allude to, or otherwise express themselves without offending censors, both official and unofficial, Buñuel's mastery of surprise, irony, wit, and subtle manipulation of detail so as to make clear what cannot be stated directly became the supreme model.

Three instances of Buñuelian handling of novels by young directors come to mind: Angelino Fons's *La busca* (1966), in which the deeply conservative Pío Baroja's portrayal of hardships of urban life in Madrid in 1904 is recast to underscore the abysmal lack of collective concern for human welfare; and Pedro Olea's *Tormento* (1974), whose nineteenth-century heroine, originally drawn by Galdós, is interpreted from the twentieth-century point of view. The most recent free adaptation of a famous novel for the screen along Buñuelian lines is Ricardo Franco's *Pascual Duarte* (1976). Camilo José Cela's ferocious, repugnant novel of provincial Spain in the 1940s is superbly altered in time and detail so as to recreate the tone of Cela's novel with a stronger voice of protest.

It was Buñuel who was able to lead Spanish directors past neorealism, an early model which proved to be useless under the constant siege of censorship. Spanish directors hoped to emulate the Italian neorealist example of revealing postwar life. Yet the direct statements and openly critical attitudes of directors such as Rossellini, De Sica, and Visconti were simply not possible in Franco's Spain. Spanish films made in the neorealist style, such as Nieves Conde's *Surcos* and Marco Ferreri's *El pisito*, that deal with social problems were heavily censored. Buñuel had never been comfortable with neorealism. As a documentarist himself, he had long preceded neorealist techniques with *Las Hurdes* in 1932. But, for a surrealist such as Buñuel, neorealism was incomplete: "reasonable, but poetry, mystery . . . are completely nonexistent."² In *Los olvidados* (1950), for example, Buñuel relies on many documentary techniques but characteristically contradicts them with scenes of visions and nightmares. Thus Buñuel's works have a lyrical quality never achieved by neorealism. It is this lyrical, metaphorical character, often vague because it conveyed inner desires surrealists considered to be the driving force of human behavior, that the young directors of the New Spanish Cinema found might be the key to subverting censorship.

Buñuel's work, of course, was among the most heavily censored in postwar Spain so it was almost unknown there for many years. *Viridiana,* made in Spain in 1960–1961, was not released there until two years after Franco's death, in 1977. In 1963, Buñuel returned to Spain briefly to play the role of an executioner in Saura's *Llanto por un bandido.* But his own films, especially those made in Mexico, had not been released in Spain. *Simón del desierto* (*Simon of the Desert*) and *Fantasma de la libertad* (*Phantom of Liberty*) were both banned. His name was eliminated from books on film, such as Fernando Méndez-Leite's multivolume *Historia del cine español* (1965), which contains no reference to Spain's greatest film director.

Just across the border, the film festivals of Perpignan and Montpellier revealed to Spanish viewers what could only be rumored in Spain. In 1958, Saura attended a conference on Hispanic film in Montpellier where he saw Buñuel's *Él* and *Subida al cielo* (*Mexican Busride*). Two years later, when *Los golfos* was sent to Cannes, Saura met Buñuel there. Gradually, Buñuel's films began to be shown at sporadic and semiprivate screenings at the National Film School and at art theaters in Madrid and Barcelona. To contend, as Peter Besas does, that Buñuel's influence on Spanish filmmakers was "minimal" disregards the impact he clearly left on some of Spain's best directors, as they readily admit.³

What Buñuel represents in Spanish film may be best described by young director Basilio Martín Patino who, in his introduction to the published script of his *Nueve cartas a Berta,* wrote the following homage:⁴

*Hubo una vez un hombre enviado por el demonio, que se llamó San Luis Buñuel. Pienso que con él, con nuestro único "homo cinematograficus" fruto de estos páramos, de estas historias, bajo estos techos racionalmente angostos, ante esta imposibilidad católica de ser, con sus huidas y sus semirregresos, con su lejanía y con su multipresencia, desde la universal Calanda a la pequeña burguesía de las cinematecas de Paris, dió de sí nuestro cinema todo lo que podía dar.*

(There was once a man, sent by the devil, called San Luis Buñuel. I think that with him, our only "homo cinematographicus," fruit of these barren plains, of their history, beneath these roofs with their meager share of reason, faced with this catholic impossibility of being, with his flights and semireturns, his distance and his multipresence, from the universal Calanda to the petty bourgeois film libraries of Paris, our cinema gave all it could give.")

Buñuel was able to do what many Spanish film directors would like to have done: that is, to have revealed their national identity and reality in images strong enough to capture the world's imagination. For, in Buñuel's films, the world becomes Spanish. Tristana is every exploited young woman who desires independence, while don Lope still lurks in the heart of male supervisors who secretly hope to savor their female protégée's physical treasures. The donkey carcasses on the piano in *Chien andalou* have become a world-famous image of decay. Finally, in contrast to most of what was filmed during Franco's dictatorship, Buñuel's Spain is authentic. The husband in *Él* who appears to be ready to sew up his wife as she sleeps can be traced back to the murderous husbands of Calderón's seventeenth-century honor tragedies. The legend of Saint James in *La vía láctea* (*The Milky Way*) is just as Buñuel tells it—the saint's bones having been lost long ago does not keep pilgrims from trekking to Santiago de Compostela. The troupe of beggars in *Viridiana* was selected from the beggar population of Toledo and Madrid. Nazarín, the outcast, is a typical anarchistic Spanish clergyman, many of whom were murdered as Communist sympathizers during the Civil War.

Buñuel's films are a rich cultural heritage from which flows a visual language as deeply rooted in Spanish tradition as that of Goya. Little wonder that they have become almost mythical to young Spanish directors. And nowhere is Buñuel's influence stronger than in the work of Spain's best postwar director, Carlos Saura.

# 8. Carlos Saura

Among postwar film directors in Spain, Saura is the most direct heir of Buñuel's film style and cultural perceptions. Saura was born January 4, 1932, in Huesca. He spent most of the Civil War years in Madrid and Barcelona. Like the rest of Spain, Saura's family was deeply split. Saura remembers the confusion this division inspired in him as a child: "Yo era realmente un exilado. Nunca terminé de entender por qué . . . los buenos eran los malos y los malos eran los buenos." (I was really an exile. I never understood why . . . the good were the bad and the bad were the good).[1]

In 1952, Carlos, who already had gained considerable experience as a still photographer, took the suggestion of his older brother and well-known painter Antonio and enrolled in the National Film School. His first professional directing job came in 1958 when he filmed a forty-five-minute travel documentary in color on the provincial village of Cuenca, where he had spent summers as a boy. He began his career with the neo-realist goal of filming testimony of postwar misery and manipulations of life under Franco. Yet, both his early successes, *Los golfos* and *La caza*, were censored. Unable to reveal Spanish life directly, Saura drew upon Buñuel's legacy of the "surreal documentary" and learned to convey reality indirectly so as to discredit the distortions of the Franco myth. He devised highly metaphorical film images and syntax which censors, confused by them, assumed would not be understood by anyone else.

Saura's metaphorical film language, however, confused the public a good deal less than it did the censors. Right-wing militants firebombed a theater in Barcelona in an attempt to steal offending frames from *La prima Angélica*. Public reaction to this film, one of Saura's best, challenged censorship and gave rise to a spontaneous national debate on the importance and place of dissident views. Criticized by both right and left wing alike, Saura, by his ability to infuriate, inherited Buñuel's role of the troublemaker whose films disturbed the uneasy calm of the "peace of Franco."

Saura began his career in the realistic idiom with *Los golfos* (*The*

*Drifters*) (1959). Filming in the ugly urban landscape of Madrid's Legazpi market, Saura focused upon a band of young criminals that preyed on the surrounding lower-class neighborhood. Juan and his five cohorts steal produce from the market, tools from trucks, or anything they can get their hands on. One of the few careers accessible to uneducated males in Spain is bullfighting and Juan, supported by his friends, who see him as a possible breadwinner for them, begins training as a matador. His friends watch him work in the bullring, wondering if they should not leave Spain to seek a better future in America.

*Los golfos* captures without pretense the desperation of a group of youths whose lives go nowhere. They support the aspirations of Juan, their only hope, by repeated theft. To fund the bullfight which Juan must enter as a novice, they rob a factory. Their hopes are high as they dress Juan in his *traje de luces* (suit of lights) and tell him "Pareces alguien" (You look like somebody). But one day before the fight, Paco is recognized by one of his robbery victims. To escape, the young man dives into a manhole. His body is discovered days later near the river.

Paco's fate foreshadows the bullfight during which Juan, unnerved by the presence of policemen at the ring, drops his cape. His moment of truth is not a deft single stroke but a badly bungled slaughter of the huge animal whose life oozes out on the sand before a booing crowd. Failing his comrades, Juan sinks his face in his hands. As in Buñuel's *Los olvidados,* which Saura had not seen, death and despair reward the high hopes of underprivileged youth. "It's difficult to be somebody here," laments one of the drifters. Spanish officialdom felt threatened by this remark and cut it from the dialogue. Saura was reprimanded by official classification of his first effort as a film of limited distribution.

The chastened young director decided that in his next film, *Llanto por un bandido* (*Lament for a Bandit*) (1963), he would follow the industry example of alluding to current reality through historical extravaganza, only, of course, the view of reality would counter the Franco mythology. *Llanto por un bandido* is a period piece that evokes the life of a nineteenth-century Andalusian bandit, José María Hinojosa, known as "El Temperanillo." In scenes that were to become standard fare in dozens of later chorizo Westerns, the bandit and his gang terrorize the Sierra Morena. When a liberal friend inspires in "El Temperanillo" a social conscience the bandit begins to support the liberal cause against the monarchists. Soon, however, a monarchist general persuades the embittered bandit to betray his cause. On his way to confront his liberal friend, "El Temperanillo" is mysteriously shot.

Within tales of internecine feuds and treason, Saura makes analogies with *franquista* politics in which the bandits are vaguely equated with the maquis, unrepatriated Republican soldiers who, like outlaws, lived at the

Alfredo Mayo (*left*) and Emilio Gutiérrez Caba (*holding dummy*) in Carlos Saura's *La caza* (1965).

margins of society after the Civil War. The monarchists are nineteenth-century versions of Franco's fascists, an analogy easily recognizable, since Franco stood for conservative principles, some unchanged since the nineteenth century.

Doubtless, the scene in which Buñuel, playing the role of executioner, and playwright Antonio Buero Vallejo as a lawyer executing six victims would have caused a sensation had it not been cut and destroyed by censors. Despite its commercial failure, however, *Llanto* is an important moment in Saura's career: it is the point at which he mastered the censors' own game. Having learned to speak through historical analogy, however, was not enough for Saura who, in his next film, devised his own political metaphors.

Moving from banditry to a war film requires only costume updating, but Saura's *La caza* (*The Hunt*) (1965) is not an ordinary war film. It is, instead, a war allegory whose central motif is a hunt. The action of *La caza* is so carefully structured that tension rises relentlessly toward its inevitable but still surprising fatal outcome. With this, his third film, Saura achieved the wide success that had eluded him and began to be recognized as Spain's most promising director.

The hunters, Paco, José, and Luis, have not seen each other in eight years. The three are middle-class businessmen, representatives of the class who won the Spanish Civil War. Together with Paco's young brother-in-law Enrique they meet on José's estate to hunt rabbits. (Probably alluding to the famous hunt scene in Jean Renoir's *Rules of the Game*. Saura wanted to call this film *The Rabbit Hunt* but was prohibited by censorship.) Juan, the gamekeeper, is their guide. A member of the working class who limps, he represents the peasant, the ultimate loser of the Civil War. He lives in a ruined shack with his senile mother and his teenage niece Carmen. The old woman lies on a cot worrying about her pets, two ferrets, which are also good rabbit hunters.

Like the second movement of a carefully structured sonata, the prehunt ritual introduces central motifs and creates foreboding as guns are cleaned and sights straightened. Talk of survival of the fittest accompanies close shots of ammunition. References to the Civil War ("Many of our Rebels were killed by faulty Lugers") are codes identifying the hunters as supporters of Franco. Their conversation is punctuated by the excessive violence for which the Franco regime was infamous. Overkill is suggested by a shot of a thistle-head blown off in target practice (a shot recalling Buñuel's *Diary of a Chambermaid*, in which M. Rebour's target is a butterfly hovering over flowers).

The war analogy is unmistakable as the hunt begins. The camera, from below, focuses on four men carrying rifles appearing in a long shot over the rise of a hill. Looming over the hill as they stalk their prey, they also signify nationalist infantrymen as hunters. They advance to the sound of loud drum rolls. The enemy/prey, rabbits, dart frantically in front of the advancing hunters, who concentrate all their middle-class frustration and anxiety on relentless slaughter. The camera catches each victim's agony as it is hit by bullets and dies squealing. Only the gamekeeper, Juan, hunts for food. The cruelty of this scene culminates in the posthunt photograph in which the hunters line up holding their kill as if celebrating the completion of a dangerous mission.

Tension relaxes during the posthunt conversation. On a walk, the men discover the skeleton of a war victim in an old bomb shelter nearby. Yet as talk turns from the past to current problems, tension begins to rise again. Paco is played by Alfredo Mayo, the tall blond actor who epitomized the *franquista* hero in numerous "approved" war movies of the 1940s. Now, in a natural extension of his earlier roles, he plays a self-satisfied industrialist married to a wealthy wife. José (Ismael Merlo) and Luis (José María Prada) have dissolved their business partnership and José hits Paco for a loan. He is insulted when, instead, Paco offers to help him find a job.

Enrique and Luis drive to a nearby village where they watch a goat being skinned. This grisly scene foreshadows approaching violence, as does the discarded tailor's dummy which the men find and take back to camp for target practice. While listening to a radio they talk of the past, when people ate rats during the Civil War. Over the radio a voice narrates a story of a man who, dreaming he is being killed by dogs, shouts, "The blood on that shirt can't be washed out!" The radio voice, a sign of other unseen voices, suggests by analogy the dreams of José, who lies sleeping close by. He is dreaming, this scene suggests, of the violent images voiced on the radio. This is confirmed by his anger when Luis wakes him up. Furious at being disturbed, José punches Luis and knocks him down. Later, José puts one of the ferrets down a rabbit-hole and Paco deliberately kills the agile creature as it reappears, a metaphor for the inevitable conversion of hunter into prey.

Hostile comments and arguments now sour the hunt. It is no surprise when the men turn on each other. Paco stands up to shoot a rabbit and is shot in the face by José. Luis drives the jeep at José, who fires at him. The dying Luis finishes off José, while the young Enrique, who personifies the postwar generation, runs off horrified. The climate of warfare created by hunting and quarreling leads inescapably to mutual slaughter in a film which finally visualizes the barely concealed ferocity and terror of life in the Franco era.

From the topic of the Spanish Civil War, imbued with its own mythology by the Franco regime, Saura turns to look at another source of conflict in Spanish society—relations between men and women. In three films—*Peppermint frappé* (1967), *Stress es tres, tres* (1968), and *La madriguera* (1969)—Saura examines the attitudes of three professional men— Julián, the radiologist in *Peppermint*, Fernando, the architect in *Stress*, and Pedro, the technocrat in *La madriguera*—and their female partners. In each of them Saura finds men and women to be so infantile that relations between them are almost inevitably disastrous.

Julián (José Luis López Vásquez) of *Peppermint frappé,* for example, is a doctor for whom women in general appear to be objects. He is looking for his ideal wife. The first scene of the film shows him cutting pictures of female faces and legs from a fashion magazine, a visual metaphor for the unrealistic, hopelessly doomed attitude of selecting a perfect spouse. Unexpectedly, Julián discovers his ideal not in a magazine but in Elena, the wife of his best friend, Pablo. Julián accompanies Elena to a beauty salon where he becomes fascinated with the world of false eyelashes, false fingernails, and wigs. Elena is played by Geraldine Chaplin who, with the deft gestures of a comedienne, enhances this serious role.

The artificial world of cosmetics reinforces the view of women as objects which runs throughout the fabric of Spanish society and signifies the belief that women can be treated as things. Like dolls, women can be painted, undressed, and so easily manipulated that some males are tempted to conclude they are not real people. That this is Julián's view of women is clear when he begins to encourage his timid medical assistant Ana to look and act like the more sophisticated Elena. Ana, whose temperament is exactly the opposite of Elena's, is also played by Geraldine Chaplin. This talented actress is able to enlarge the film by emphasizing the differences between the two women she portrays.

At first, Julián's fixation, like Fernando's jealousy in Buñuel's *Él*, seems to be an entirely normal attitude, no different from that of any man who encourages his partner to "fix herself up." But soon his desire to change Ana becomes obsessive. After work one evening he prepares Ana a peppermint frappé and asks her why she doesn't wear makeup. He places her on his rowing machine and calls out rowing strokes until the bewildered young woman is exhausted. The pathological consequences of Julián's obsession surface only when, intent on remaking Ana, he neatly kills Elena and Pablo so that Ana can assume her role as Elena's replica without interference from the original model and her husband.

If the characters of *Peppermint* are engulfed by Julián's pathological attitudes toward women, pathology and its resulting violence hover just below the surface of Saura's next film, *Stress es tres, tres (Three's a Crowd)*. *Stress* is a study of male jealousy in which tension builds much the same way as in *La caza*. Teresa, her husband, and his friend Antonio go on an outing together to the beach. At first Teresa is brusquely excluded by Fernando from the business conversation he is having with his friend. He is irritated by her efforts to participate in their chat and tells her, "No es cosa tuya" (It doesn't concern you). They make a stop by Aunt Mathilde's country home where, in a moment of privacy, Fernando makes amorous moves toward Teresa. She resists and Fernando immediately suspects that Teresa is thinking of Antonio. Only a few hours separate Fernando's feelings of camaraderie from the hostility and suspicion he now holds toward Antonio.

Teresa resents Fernando's treatment of her, yet she is diffident and keeps to herself the thoughts she has of standing up to him. When they arrive at the beach, however, she leaves the fuming Fernando on the shore, drinking, while she goes snorkling with Antonio. Soon Fernando puts on his wet suit and follows them. A long shot reveals him stabbing the sand with his dart-gun, venting his pent-up rage. But when he catches sight of Teresa giving Antonio a friendly kiss, Fernando leaves the water and goes ashore to reload his dart gun. Sinister music accompanies this scene, and violence seems inevitable. Instead we see Fernando's wishful vision of shooting Antonio with his dart gun while his rival, full of arrows like the martyred Saint Sebastian, falls dead on the sand. Fernando instead breaks up the party, packs their belongings, and drives them home. The camera focuses on the car in a long shot as it disappears in the distance, suggesting that the unresolved tension Fernando takes home with him can only be released violently.

In the last of this triptych, *La madriguera (The Den)*, Saura examines how men and women learn the destructive behavior that defeats them. He reveals how the roles people play as children carry over into adulthood and are, in the case of the couple in this film, Teresa (Geraldine Chaplin) and Pedro (Per Oscarssen), never entirely outgrown. The pair are members of the rich bourgeoisie who do not have to depend on anyone for their needs. They dismiss their servants, ignore their friends, and, in their concrete home, live isolated lives out of range of prying eyes.

Pedro and Teresa amuse themselves by playing games in which they re-enact roles they learned in childhood. As in some forms of psychotherapy they invest real, often intense emotion in their games. In one scene they enact a father/daughter sequence in which Teresa, acting and speaking as a little girl (she calls him Papá), is summoned by her father, played by Pedro dressed in his business suit and seated at his desk. He asks her why she does such strange things and admonishes her for lack of diligence by pulling up her skirt and spanking her with a ruler. This punishment is related directly to the impact of a paternalistic religion on her childhood, for now Teresa kneels, hands folded, and begins to sing. The submission of the child to her father is now repeated in a religious context, where the little girl kneels before an angry God who threatens her with a fiery sword. These childhood reenactments help explain the submissive attitudes of the adult Teresa.

After the religious scene, both partners assume their child roles. Pedro imitates a dog and begins to bark. Teresa brings him a dish of raw meat. As games often do, this one becomes suddenly serious and destructive. Teresa, surprised when Pedro growls and bites her ankle, picks up a broom and clobbers him. The game ends with Pedro nursing a bleeding lip and the exhausted Teresa lying down on her bed looking up at photos of some big-time role players—the pope, Marlon Brando, and other movie stars.

Although Pedro has all the high-tech diversions, he often gets bored playing with his computer, stereo, television, and tape recorder. He is amused by his wife's games and is drawn into them by her, but she is a more compulsive player and he is often unable to tell when she is playing and when she is being serious. One evening before dinner he hears a shot and discovers Teresa lying on the floor bleeding from the temple. He reaches for the phone but stops, suspecting a game. Sure enough, he spots a bottle of ketchup nearby and gives her a stern look.

As Françoise Aude points out, Pedro is a father figure whom Teresa both loves and hates.[2] She has never grown up fully and still relates to men as she did to her father and to the priest in childhood. Now she is irritated at Pedro's refusal to play her current game. She rebels by carrying the game too far and Pedro becomes a victim of her vengeance. By far the most intriguing and complex of the triptych, *La madriguera* suggests that all is not well in the family den or lair which produces characters such as Pedro and Teresa. As the idle rich they represent fascism itself, as Robert Phillip Kolker describes it—"the dark side of bourgeois complacency and self-centeredness." [3]

In these intimate portraits of male/female interactions filmed during the late 1960s, Saura gathers the evidence he uses for his political metaphors of the early 1970s. Generations of sexual repression by the church, purchase of protection from social responsibility by the bourgeoisie, and denial of professional roles to women by society produce in the 1960s triptych individual character distortions that later erupt in collective psychoses in his 1970s films. Seeking links between individual and collective behavior, Saura develops his political metaphors in the context of the predominant unit of social organization, the middle-class family. Another reason Saura chooses the family as context for his political memoirs is that the Spanish conflict was a Civil War in which families were split, brothers conspired against each other, and personal identities were fragmented by political division. The childhood games in *La madriguera* are, like the psychodramas of *El jardín de las delicias* (*The Garden of Delights*) (1970), ways in which adults relive the past.

*Jardín* is the first of the series of political allegories for which Saura is best known. They are a skillful blend of metaphor which Saura learned to master in *La caza,* set within the context of family life. In them, reference to the family signifies both domestic and national life. Just as *La caza* refers to the tenor of Spanish post–Civil War life as a hunt, in *Jardín* Franco's Spain is personified by a Spanish industrialist, Antonio Cano, who has lost his memory in an auto accident. Antonio, head of his family's cement factory, is like Spain throughout half the twentieth century— he has no voice and is paralyzed. He is at the mercy of his greedy family who, like the fascist bureaucracy during the *franquista* period, tried to profit from an ailing economy. The "delights" of the title refers to a series of tableaux, like Bosch's painting of the same name, in which family members enact a series of psychodramas in hopes that Antonio will recall his Swiss bank account number.

Antonio's family tries to recreate scenes from his past, beginning with the cruel punishment, inflicted upon him at age five, of being locked in the closet with a huge pig that, his father warns, will eat his feet and hands. Family members, dressed in 1930s styles and playing music of the era, watch intently as the adult Antonio is wheeled from the closet. But instead of recalling the past, Antonio has collapsed in a dead faint. Next they stage his first communion, which occurred in 1931. They hire soldiers who, in costume, break into the chapel and interrupt the ritual, shouting, "¡Viva la República! ¡Viva Jesús Hernández!" (Hernández was editor of a leftist newspaper). War planes buzz overhead and shots are fired as the confused amnesia victim stands, shouts, and ducks at the sound of gunfire.

Especially transparent is a staged hunt, recalling innumerable hunts Franco himself arranged to impress important visitors. Friends place a shotgun in Antonio's hands and a bird is released into the air. Antonio aims, fires, and the bird falls. But when the mangled bird is dumped into his lap, Antonio discovers a wire attached to its leg and realizes that the hunt has been contrived. Other images of hunting disturb Antonio; medieval armored cavalry gallop toward him suddenly one afternoon in the garden. He takes refuge in wife Luchy's bedroom, where a framed picture of the same horsemen hangs over the wall safe. The armed warriors signify the rich bourgeoisie who won the Civil War and inherited the nation's wealth. They now pursue money with the same zeal with which they vanquished their Republican enemies.

Antonio is taken to the family archives where photographs line the walls. He listens to a tape recording of his own voice, made before his accident, addressing a family business meeting. His authoritative tone and the responding applause inspire him to memorize the same speech for delivery at a board meeting where he hopes to regain his position as head of the corporation. His memory fails, however, and the board votes to declare him insane.

The family finds that they cannot restore by trauma a memory which has become unrestorable. In the final tableau, two wrecked cars sit locked in a head-on collision in the garden. The camera closes in on the bloody bodies strewn about. Antonio, now a victim of a reenactment of his near fatal crash, mutters from the wreckage, "Do what you want with my body, but don't let them touch my head." As in *Death of a Cyclist*, the camera closes in on the maimed crash victim, but Saura holds this shot longer on the screen. Antonio realizes that without his mind, of which memory is a vital part, his body is useless. Like Spain, Antonio is unable to understand himself or his own history. Suddenly a wheelchair passes behind him, followed by another.

On the sound track, an a cappella male chorus sings a triumphant cantata. The camera, tracking back, reveals the garden crossed in all directions by family members in wheelchairs. As Saura's hunters became prey in *La caza*, the victors of the Civil War themselves become staring amnesia victims in *Jardín*. Without vital information about their past (information about the Civil War was officially repressed by the Franco regime), they remain paralyzed, unable to participate in contemporary life.

The uncomprehending face of loss in *Jardín* and the later *La prima Angélica* is that of José Luis López Vásquez, an actor of incomparable versatility. As Alfredo Mayo came to typify the *franquista* hero in the cinema of official mythology, López Vásquez achieves an almost iconographic importance in the countermyths of Carlos Saura. The talented actress Luchy Soto also performs repeatedly in Saura's films. She hones to perfection the role of indignant wife in *Jardín, Ana y los lobos,* and *Mamá cumple cien años.*

### Ana y los lobos (Ana and the Wolves) (1972)

Saura's next grim parable presents an analogy of Spain as a daft, sinister family that lives in a huge mansion totally isolated from any contact with civilization. It is inhabited by three brothers, the lobos, who personify the obsessions in which Spanish culture is rooted: José (José María Prada), the military macho, the sexually repressed Juan (José Vivo), and Fernando (Fernando Fernán Gómez), the religious fanatic. At the center of this sinister trio is their mother, Mamá, a huge, infantile woman who can only move out of bed with assistance. This role is enacted with amazing vitality by the irrepressible octogenarian Rafaela Aparicio.

Into the wolves' lair wanders Ana, a foreign tutor, whose naiveté Geraldine Chaplin portrays with a careful balance between the well-meaning but slightly fey young adventurer. She arrives packing the toys of European technology—hair dryer and tape recorder—in her bags, underscoring her non-Spanish identity. She will serve as governess to Juan and his wife Luchy's three young girls. Ignorant and trusting, Ana seems to represent the hapless seekers of fortune who enter Spanish culture with no conception of its history or problems.

She is fresh meat for the pack, and it closes in on her. José introduces himself as the paterfamilias and inspects her passport and suitcase. Juan writes her obscene letters posted with foreign stamps from the family stamp collection. Fernando ignores her as he busily whitewashes a nearby cave into which he prepares to move. But when she visits his cave and dozes off he tries to cut her hair as she lies sleeping.

The three wolves were raised by an indulgent mother who is now bedridden and suffers mysterious fainting spells. She complains about the confusion that reigns in the house ("todo en esta casa está desordenada") but she blames this on the Civil War—"antes de la guerra no era así" (before the war it wasn't like this). Yet it is she who has kept her sons from maturing by nurturing their obsessions. When José confesses to her that he is in love with Ana, Mamá advises, "Ponte un uniforme y te sentirás mucho más seguro" (Put on a uniform and you'll feel more secure). José, who is still unable to read, replies, "Mamá, tú eres la única que me entiende" (You're the only one who understands me).

Satire of Spain's military establishment is one of the major themes in *Ana y los lobos*. José, whose fixation with authoritarianism is conveyed with uncanny skill by the late actor José María Prada, invites the amazed Ana to his "*museo,*" where male mannequins display his favorite military uniforms. He puts on a record of march music and begins unpacking his latest uniform. "It must be nice to wear a uniform and order other people around," teases Ana. A paper bird flutters down mysteriously and José takes out his pistol and shoots it several times. "Bravo," sneers Ana, who walks out, leaving José in full uniform with pistol in hand, angry at being ridiculed. The violent outcome of this madness is foreshadowed when Juan's three daughters bring Ana a doll they have found buried in the mud. "Ha sido los lobos," they tell her. "Han cortado su pelo" (It was the wolves . . . they cut her hair). When Ana asks Fernando who tortured the doll, he replies that José did it. The doll, of course, is a substitute for Ana, who shares the same fate.

In a preposterous final scene, Luchy, on top of the roof, screams her complaints about Juan, who watches porno movies. Mamá declares that Ana must go. Ana goes to her room and turns off her tape recorder, a move suggesting that these fantasies in Spain are reality that can be recorded, thus making *Ana y los lobos* a kind of horror documentary, a genre that begins with Buñuel's *Las Hurdes.*

Ana sets forth into the vacant fields that surround the house, but she is ambushed by the brothers, who, although they have plotted against each other, now cooperate in the brutal destruction of the foreign tutor: Juan rapes her, Fernando cuts her hair, and José handcuffs her and shoots her with his pistol. Like Spain, this devouring family destroys foreign elements which do not fit into its culture. Isolated and complacent, its institutions have assumed monstrous proportions. *Ana y los lobos* recalls Goya's caption to one of the prints in *Los caprichos* which warns that "the sleep of reason produces monsters." Another *capricho,* picturing a huge woman flying through the air, is the source of the sequel *Mamá cumple cien años.* Fernando quotes Goya's caption of this *capricho* when he explains one day, "Mamá es hidrópica" (Mamá's got dropsy).[4]

## La prima Angélica (Cousin Angélica) (1973)

Saura established a link between his films of political memoirs, so that each work seems to be a page from a family album. A cousin of the monsters in *Ana* who is mentioned in passing in that film becomes a central

Luis ( José Luis López Vásquez) remembers his parents in Carlos Saura's *La prima Angélica* (1973).

figure in one of Saura's best-known and, for Spaniards, most scandalous films, *La prima Angélica.*

The protagonist of *La prima Angélica* is Luis (José Luis López Vásquez), an editor who lives in Barcelona. He makes a painful journey to honor his mother's wishes that her remains lie in her home town, near Madrid. His return to the village, where his Aunt Pilar (Josefina Díaz) still lives, is also a trip into the past recalling uneasy memories of the Civil War. During the journey Luis sees reality on two levels—as the adult he now is and as he remembers it in his boyhood when he was Luisito. The real achievement of this film is the merging of these two levels of reality so that the child and the adult are indistinguishable and exist together in a Bergsonian *durée,* or continuum, without benefit of flashbacks.

Taking his clues from Buñuel, who stressed the force of dreams by photographing them on the same level of perception as daily reality, Saura emphasizes the power of the past by juxtaposing scenes from Luis's boyhood with those of his current life without distinguishing between them. The Model T Ford that makes its way down a lonely highway toward the camera is the visual clue that Luis is both crossing the barren Castilian hills and recalling his boyhood as he does so. When the car stops, Luis's

Luis and his family gather at the cemetery in Saura's *La prima Angélica* (1973).

parents get out and try to convince him that he must stay with his relatives for the summer.

The camera cuts to Aunt Pilar's house, whose rooms and objects are all links between present and past. The taste of his aunt's hot chocolate, like Proust's *madeleine,* converts the characters at the dining table into those he knew as a boy—his grandmother, aunt, uncle, and cousin Angélica. Time switches from past to present jolt the viewer throughout the film. Angélica (Lina Canalejas), Luis's childhood sweetheart, is now a disillusioned housewife married to Anselmo, who so resembles Angélica's authoritarian, fascist father, Luis's uncle, that the same actor plays both roles.

One afternoon Luis accompanies Angélica, Anselmo (Fernando Delgado), and their young daughter (María Clara Fernández) on a weekend picnic to a patch of treeless plain where Anselmo triumphantly shows off the site of the new house and swimming pool he plans to build. Luis is distracted from Anselmo's complacent chatter by visions of his boyhood. He shows Angélica's daughter the stone cross nearby with his and Angélica's names which he carved in 1938. He remembers visits to this site with his relatives. The image he recalls of Aunt Pilar, Angélica's mother, his uncle, and his grandmother walking together is the scene which infu-

Luis ties young Angélica's braid in Saura's *La prima Angélica* (1973).

riated conservatives and, in turn, opened for public discussion the topic of the Civil War. For Uncle Anselmo's arm, wounded in battle, is bandaged in a cast that extends in front of him, signifying a permanently stiff fascist salute.

Further offensive images included Luis's vision of a wartime visit to another aunt, a nun who, apparently recovering from an act of mortification, sits soaking her hand in a pan of water. Family members visiting with the nun are accompanied by Anselmo, who sits across the table with his conspicuously bandaged arm. These images, associating an obsessive church with a rigid fascism, were easily recognized as codes ridiculing the supporters of and believers in the Franco mythology. Filmed only two years before Franco's death, they caused a furor in the national press, which received letters calling for the destruction of this extraordinary film.

While the character of Anselmo does not change as he switches roles from uncle to husband, Luis's female relatives alter in appearance from present to past. Luis, too, remains the same, a technique intended to stress the extent to which the child still acts within the adult of the present. An example is the scene in which Luis and Angélica spend a few moments together poring over their old school notebooks in the attic. Captivated by renewed friendship, the two climb out on the roof and sit side by side, reminiscing. Luis turns to kiss Angélica's hair when suddenly, as in his boyhood, the voice of her father, Anselmo, booms out angrily demanding that he come down. The authoritarian voice calls again, this time for Angélica. But when Anselmo enters the attic in search of Luis and Angélica, it is Angélica's young daughter who climbs back through the window, thus defining without flashbacks the present as an uninterrupted continuation of the past.

Luis discovers his present identity in recollections of his boyhood. When he gives Angélica's daughter a bicycle ride, he recalls his own attempt, many years ago, to escape to Madrid on his bike with Angélica. The humiliation of the beating his uncle gave him still remains, for the camera focuses on the adult Luis, kneeling as the angry Uncle Anselmo whips him. This image of the adult Luis in fetal position before Anselmo signifies not only personal defeat but also, on a national level, the postwar vengeance of the victorious fascists.

The boy's punishment by his uncle, compounded by loss of the Civil War, saps the adult Luis's confidence, so that when Angélica, sad and lonely, approaches him for consolation one day in the kitchen, Luis remains passive and begins to plan his departure. As he leaves, Aunt Pilar begins to tell Luis to send her love to his father, a Republican and thus an enemy during the Civil War. But she stops short, silenced by the enmity that still divides the family after forty years.

*Angélica* ends by extending forty years of defeat and conflict into the present and, inevitably, the future, for Angélica's unanswered question of many years ago still haunts Luis: "Tu padre . . . ¿qué ha hecho? La abuela estaba muy triste porque decía que cuando los nacionales tomen Madrid, igual lo fusilan" (What did your father do? Grandmother was very sad because she said when the nationalists take Madrid, the first thing they'll do is shoot him).[5] By not changing the protagonist into a child, Saura makes clear the extent to which the fear cast by this remark into the nine-year-old still lives within the adult Luis.

Hoping to calm the outrage his film aroused, Saura stressed the psychoanalytic rather than the political context of *Angélica:* "No estoy diciendo nada nuevo. Ya lo han dicho Adler, Jung, y Marcuse. Soy un resonador de ellos" (I'm not saying anything new. Adler, Jung, and Marcuse have already said it. I am only echoing them).[6] But this disclaimer did not distract public attention from the political meaning of *Angélica*. Many Spaniards recognized Luis's search for identity as their own in this film, one of the biggest box office hits as well as one of the most disturbing of the Franco dictatorship.

### Cría cuervos (1975)

Juan Goytisolo, one of Spain's best-known postwar writers, has explained that the frequent occurrence of children as narrators or central characters in Spanish novels of the postwar era is due to the fact that many of Spain's novelists were themselves children during the war and experienced the conflict with the partial understanding of a child. This comment helps to understand why two of Saura's most original and spontaneous works, *La prima Angélica* and *Cría cuervos,* reflect reality through the eyes of a child. If *Angélica* stresses the indelible imprint of childhood on adults, *Cría* reverses focus to capture the impact of the adult world on children.

Just as the family's cousin Angélica was mentioned by a character in *Ana y los lobos,* the title of *Cría* is repeated in *La prima Angélica.* When military police intercept Luisito and Angélica in a combat zone on the way to Madrid on their bicycle, they return the children to Angélica's father, Anselmo. As he whips Luisito, Anselmo, whose dual role personifies two generations of *franquismo,* mutters the bitter Spanish proverb, "Cría cuervos y te sacarán los ojos" (Raise ravens and they'll pluck out your eyes).

Saura's choice of a proverb for the title of this film is an accurate reflection of fascist use of language. Myths, as Roland Barthes points out, often resort to proverbs as an authoritarian form of speech that appears to be beyond question, part of a universal, natural order. The rancorous prediction of this particular proverb is especially typical of a repressive, fearful, and conformist myth such as that of the Franco regime. *Cría* is another attempt by Saura to demystify this mythology, for its protagonist, Ana, resists every attempt to initiate her into its rituals.

The action of *Cría* is seen through the eyes of Ana, nine, and her sisters Irene, eleven, and Maite, about seven. The film's most engrossing scene is its opening, in which Ana watches from the stairwell as her father's lover, obviously agitated, leaves in a hurry. She becomes increasingly annoyed when she looks up to see Ana staring at her. Ana goes in to see her father lying in bed, dead of a sudden heart attack. Ana, not at all surprised at this, looks lovingly at her father, takes a glass from the bedside table to the kitchen, and washes all traces of a white liquid from it. This creation of suspense and eye for minute detail have by now become characteristic of Saura's political memoirs.

*Cría* is another page from the family album. The father turns out to have been another authoritarian Anselmo who served in Spain's famous Division Azul, or Blue Division. The Blue Division was a volunteer division which defended the Nazis against Soviet troops in 1941. Ana scandalizes her Aunt Paulina when she refuses to kiss her bemedaled father as they pay their last respects at his funeral in the family parlor.

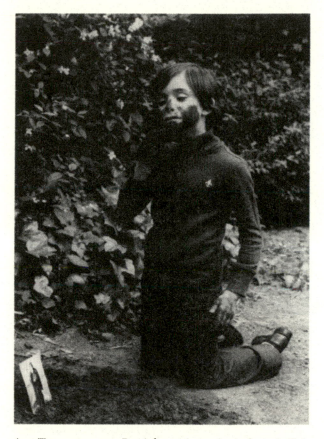

Ana Torrent mourns Roni, her guinea pig, in Saura's *Cría cuervos* (1975).

Aunt Paulina (Monica Randall) takes over the raising of the three girls, but she is no substitute for their mother, who, like Saura's own mother, chose her family over her career as a concert pianist. Ana's mother, sick in mind and body, dies of cancer in an agonizing death scene which Ana observes until she can stand her mother's screams no longer and runs out, hands over her ears. Ana's sense of loss is a major theme in the film, underscored by the melancholy song Ana and her sisters play on their phonograph entitled "¿Por qué te vas?" ("Why Are You Going Away?").

Deliberate generational confusion is created with the role of Ana. Geraldine Chaplin plays Ana's mother, a role she enacts superbly but which soon culminates in the withering death scene. She tells us in full-face narration before the camera that the child in the film is herself at age nine. The result of what Hélène Marinot has called "ce dédoublement de la

Ana Torrent and Geraldine Chaplin as Ana, from Saura's *Cría cuervos* (1975).

personage" (this bifurcation of the character)[7] is the clear implication that, as the child becomes the mother, her hopes, too, will fade since women's lives in Spain have not changed for generations.

Ana's grandmother is played by Josefina Díaz, who, as a young actress in 1933, starred in Lorca's play *Bodas de sangre* (*Blood Wedding*). Her role is a mute testament to the fact that women in a paternalistic society are not only confined as the grandmother is to her wheelchair—to the home as the only domain—but are without a voice in the Franco dictatorship. As an adult, Ana speculates whether her mother regretted abandoning her career—"Yo creo que siempre le queda . . . el resquemar de haber abandonado una profesión que podía haber sido liberadora" (I think the sting of having abandoned a profession that could have offered her opportunity is always with her)—or if she really preferred the domestic life "sin complicaciones al riesgo de una responsabilidad que no podía compartir" (without the complications of a responsibility she could not share).[8]

Ana, played with astoundingly natural demeanor by the nine-year-old Ana Torrent, has known love, loss, and hypocrisy in her short life. Her father, mother, and pet guinea pig, to whom she is very attached, all die. Only Rosa, the earth-motherly maid, remains to console her. The controlling Paulina, however, sees that Rosa remains at a distance, so Ana is without the love of an adult whom she cherishes. She shares her solitude with her two sisters, but even their childhood games and favorite song, the popular "¿Por qué te vas?" echo their loneliness and isolation.

With a child's intuitive understanding, Ana resists Paulina, who perpetuates her father's patriarchal code. She blames her father for her mother's illness, so she refuses him a farewell kiss as he lies in his coffin. Ana tries to control her world with the two items left to her by her parents—her mother's sodium bicarbonate and her father's pistol. With the white powder, which her mother assured her was a terrible poison that, in small doses, could kill an elephant, Ana prepares a drink for her father and thus assumes that it caused his death. She is amazed when Paulina wakes healthy the next morning after drinking a similar glassful at bedtime.

Pistol in hand, Ana barges into the room where Paulina and Nicolás sit talking one afternoon. Nicolás, a friend of Ana's father, has just urged Paulina to go away with him as he seeks refuge from a failing marriage. They are at first angry when Ana interrupts them but quickly take a less hostile approach to the insistent child when they find themselves gazing down the barrel of her father's pistol. This scene suggests that the patriarchal double standard, which allowed Ana's father, Anselmo, to amuse himself with maids and mistresses but left Ana's mother deeply depressed, alone, and ill, is finally challenged by a nine-year-old girl who by chance catches Nicolás in an awkward moment.

*Cría* was filmed in an old house on María de Molina Street in Madrid.[9] As in *Jardín de las delicias,* its enclosed garden has a drained swimming pool, signifying the empty reservoir of national memory. In *Jardín,* Antonio had visions of being dumped into the pool. In *Cría,* Ana plays in the dry cement reservoir as the traffic from the outside world is heard on the sound track. Ana and her sisters enter the outside world only when they go back to school after vacation.

The film ends as bells, sound of the Western religious call to worship, toll the reopening of the parochial school. A long shot of schoolgirls filing into an aging building signifies the education of Spanish women. Ana, as yet fearless of the authoritarian militaristic heritage her family represents, will be thoroughly indoctrinated in obedience and submission by the religious institution. By the time she finishes school, she and her sisters will be like the generations of Spanish women before her—with no voice to protest, like her paralyzed grandmother; confined like Paulina; or depressed, as their mother was before her death. *Cría,* filmed the year before Franco's death, thus clarifies how the regime, through an antique religious education, makes certain that the young do not mature into *cuervos*—rebels against its fascist myth.

# 9. Other Important Directors

Proustian themes and elliptical style help make Saura's films recognizable and intriguing to a European audience and have insured his success abroad. In Spain, however, Saura reaches only an educated minority and is considered to be a director who speaks to an international rather than to a primarily national public. Like Buñuel, whom Octavio Paz chided for not making his films more obviously committed to opposition of bourgeois politics,[1] Saura, too, has been criticized as a right-wing collaborator simply because he was able to continue working. This criticism is valid only to the extent that *la estética franquista* is often obscure to an uninformed public. The film language of the opposition, designed to demystify and conceal as well as reveal, never lost sight of its purpose of undermining rather than placating a hostile fascist regime.

Saura's achievement, however, has often diverted attention from the work of less well known but talented directors. The directors whose films are discussed in this chapter are those of the New Spanish Cinema who share with Saura an urgent need to reveal Spain to itself. They have in some measure succeeded, since these films are among the landmarks of postwar Spanish cinema.

## Directors of the 1960s

Miguel Picazo's *La tía Tula* (1964), a version of the novel by renowned Spanish philosopher Miguel de Unamuno, is one of the most advanced films of its decade for its treatment of the theme of social hypocrisy in the definition of woman's role in society. This hypocrisy not only implicates the male power structure based upon the church but the entire provincial culture which represents more than half of Spain. When Marco Ferreri suggested the idea of adapting *La tía Tula,* Picazo accepted at once, remembering two examples from his personal acquaintance with women who enjoy raising someone else's children while staunchly refusing to marry.

Tula sews while Ramiro dines in Miguel Picazo's *La tía Tula* (1964).

In Spain, particularly in the provinces, respectable women have in the past had two alternatives in life: they married or they entered the convent. As the church lost much of its power and prominence, the choices for women narrowed. Picazo's film opens as Tula's sister Rosa is being buried and mourned by her husband, Ramiro, and two children, whom she leaves in Tula's care. The camera at once introduces us to the severity of provincial life by focusing upon Tula, a pretty young woman dressed in black sitting in a chair against a plain white wall. At her left a solid dark wooden door is very slightly ajar, a powerful visual metaphor of the isolated, lonely, closed life of women in provincial Spain. Tula carries out her promise to Rosa to care for the children with such zeal and success that, to Ramiro, she seems the ideal wife. When he approaches the subject of marriage, however, or even tries to touch her, she reacts with extreme disdain. Tula is an intelligent woman who enjoys her life and her friends. She wants only to care for the children and to help Ramiro. She does not intend to marry and tells Ramiro early in the film, "I can't put up with a man." "How do you put up with me, then?" "You're my sister's husband."

One morning when she comes in to wake him, Ramiro tries to seduce her and she fights him off. This encounter ends all dialogue between them. Tula, having sublimated or repressed her sexuality, now sees Ramiro as an enemy. Ramiro becomes so frustrated and depressed that, on a family

Ramiro tries to convince Tula in Miguel Picazo's *La tía Tula* (1964).

visit to relatives in another town, he seduces the surprised and frightened fourteen-year-old niece, Juanita. When he and Tula take his children home they cannot find Juanita. The frightened adolescent is hiding under a bed. The question of his remarriage is resolved when Juanita becomes pregnant. Ramiro realizes that it is she, barely older than his own children, whom he must marry.

In the final sequence we see a train compartment occupied by Ramiro and what appears to be three children. But it is Ramiro and his new wife, Juanita, who, along with the two younger children, prepare to depart. Tula is bereft at the loss of her niece and nephew. She waves farewell to them, pressing her black-gloved hands against the train window in gestures of despair as the train pulls out of the station. Unmarried women in Spain fit nowhere and frequently become neurotic, depressed, or even deranged. José Monleón credits Picazo with rejecting madness as Tula's fate and with treating her not as "a Freudian monster" but as an entirely credible character emerging from her social context in which women do not have any alternatives to marriage.[2] Early in the film, the question of whether Tula is actually insane is raised. In a sequence at the cemetery, Ramiro and his son Ramín put flowers on Rosa's grave when suddenly a woman goes berserk and begins to scream, "Why did I do it?" This shrill question echoes throughout the tombs, frightening Ramín, who runs to his father. They leave and return home to the loving and competent Tula who, although unmarried, is neither berserk nor destroyed by the kind of life she has chosen.

Dark shadows and strong contrast in black and white set an appropriately stark emotional tone for this film. Tula receives no support for her decision to remain single. The priest encourages her to marry. Telling her that Ramiro's attempt to seduce her is "natural," this priest recalls the priest in Buñuel's *Él* (1953) who tells Gloria that even though her insanely jealous husband has tried to kill her she must try to understand, since "he's your husband." In a *machista* society, criminal behavior toward wives receives religious sanction in accordance with Hispanic attitudes. Any director trying to describe a normal Spanish female in defiance of these attitudes in 1964 must be considered daring and courageous. That Picazo creates characters who are fully appealing human beings developed in an interesting, direct, and simple narrative makes *La tía Tula* still very much alive today. The performances of its leading actor, Carlos Estrada, and actress Aurora Batista, are as fresh today as when they were filmed over twenty years ago.

In contrast to Tula, who is left alone because she acted upon her convictions, Lorenzo, the young protagonist of Basilio Martín Patino's *Nueve cartas a Berta* (*Nine Letters to Berta*) (1965), resigns himself almost without a fight to a stultifying existence. His ideal is Berta, to whom he writes the nine letters that form the structure of the film and are read aloud by a voice-off. But, since Berta is never seen on screen or even heard from, the entire film is not a dialogue with Berta at all but an inner monologue illustrated with scenes from Lorenzo's provincial life.

Lorenzo (Emilio Caba), a student at a provincial university, met Berta while on a trip to London. She is the daughter of a Spanish émigré, a renowned literary scholar who earns an enviable salary teaching at an American university. Lorenzo's longing for all the émigré represents—travel, money, professional achievement—is reflected in his letters to Berta. Yet he is a well-behaved, docile youth whose inner conflict is expressed by silence and by his refusal to respond to his parents when they get angry at him.

Lorenzo's restlessness never approaches anything resembling rebellion. While he struggles to resolve questions of religious faith with the local priest, Father Echarri, his friends at the university in Madrid are reading Simone de Beauvoir and Gramschi. Lorenzo's visit to his friend Jacques in Madrid is a turning point in his life. He senses that in comparison with his more sophisticated peers, he already seems isolated and somewhat repressed.

While he is wondering to Berta in a letter if being good is worth the trouble, his friend Jacques is enjoying a relationship with his French girlfriend, Simone. Jacques and Simone give him a ride back home where Lorenzo's parents, furious at the arrival of unexpected guests, receive them awkwardly. Even after Jacques and Simone hastily depart, the angry parents barely speak to Lorenzo, who, trapped between conformist parents and friends too sophisticated for him, remains miserable.

Lorenzo's inner turmoil culminates in an illness which signals not battle but resignation, for when he recovers he gives up asking himself (or Berta) questions that might lead him away from established traditions. He renews his friendship with Mary Tere (Mari Carillo), his hometown girlfriend, although he does not share with her the thoughts he wrote to Berta. Their kiss that ends the film does not produce a happy ending nor does it signify a new beginning. It represents renunciation, falsification, and silence and as such is an excellent metaphor for the *franquista* period—almost a kiss of death, which life for Lorenzo will seem in provincial Spain.

Like the life it depicts, *Nueve cartas* is slow, monotonous, and without surprise. Since we soon know what the outcome must be, the boredom of Basilio Martín Patino's film is much like that of Antonioni, which instructs by example. The protagonist who refuses to fight is distanced from the spectator by his lack of will, yet the weight of tradition and the national past upon him are almost tangible. The long shots of the ponderous architecture, even when seen at its most enchanting moments (with spotlights at night), seem interminable. Father Echarri encourages Lorenzo to remain in this archaic setting by comparing the peace of rural life to the meaningless and destructive violence of the world outside.

The same dilemma that preoccupied Unamuno and the Spanish literary Generation of 1898—"españolizarse o europeizarse" (cling to traditional Spanish ways or Europeanize)—still haunts Lorenzo. And he makes the same choice as the Spanish intellectuals who preceded him almost half a century ago. He decides to remain amid the rural society and provincial peace in which he has recuperated from his *crise de conscience*. Yet Lorenzo's peace appears an empty consolation for the lack of intellectual stimulation. It represents life on the receding outer margins of a past century. *Nueve cartas* is an almost excruciating experience of the silence and tedium of that life.

Lorenzo's existential conflict with his Spanish family, tradition, and faith pales beside the more basic struggle for survival waged by the young protagonist of Angelino Fons's *La busca* (*The Search*) (1966). Although Manuel fails for much the same reason as Lorenzo (a lack of will to fight), Lorenzo's questions are the bourgeois ones of whether or not to accept his culture. Unlike Lorenzo, Manuel has no choices. His is a life-and-death battle within the social and historical context of his country and the personal circumstances of poverty and ignorance that paralyze him.

The historical dimensions of the film are sketched in a brief documentary prologue accompanied by the following voice-off narrative.

*Al acabar el siglo XIX, España despertó del hermoso sueño de la Restauración, un sueño que había emergido con la coronación de Alfonso XII. Los hombres de la Restauración creyeron, de buena fe, haber acabado para siempre con las luchas fratricidas que habían durado más de 50 años. Creyeron haber garantizado a España un futuro de progreso y felicidad. El llamado "desastre colonial," como un grito, pulverizó todas estas ilusiones. Nuestro país, sin colonias, con una agricultura social y técnicamente atrasada, con una industria débil, con una población en constante aumento, se enfrentaba con el mundo moderno en las peores condiciones que cabe imaginar. Parecía que el mundo avanzaba y nosotros estábamos parados. En este medio se centra la historia de Manuel, adolescente que inició su "lucha por la vida" en aquel momento histórico. Para él, como para su patria, el futuro sólo era un mezcla de amenaza, incertidumbre, y confusión.*

(At the end of the nineteenth century, Spain awoke from the lovely dream that was the Restoration, a dream which had emerged with the coronation of Alfonso XII. The men of the Restoration believed, in good faith, that they had put an end forever to the civil strife that had lasted more than 50 years. They thought they had guaranteed Spain a felicitous and progressive future. The so-called colonial disaster shattered, like a scream, these illusions. Our country, without colonies, with a socially and technologically backward agriculture, weak industry, and constantly increasing population, confronted the modern world in the worst imaginable conditions. It seemed that the world was progressing and we were stuck. Against this background is set the story of Manuel, a youth who began his "struggle for life" at that historical moment. For him, as for his country, the future was only a mixture of threats, uncertainty, and confusion.)

This grim but accurate narration of Spain's historical predicament becomes personal history when the camera, after juxtaposing scenes of bread lines and royal receptions, views of dress parades with shots of the Valencian rice fields and primitive agricultural laborers, focuses at last on a photo of three small boys and zooms in on one of them. Next we see a young man, Manuel (Jacques Perrin), just arrived in Madrid, and his mother, expertly portrayed by Lola Gaos, walking to the *pensión* where she works. Manuel's character is quickly sketched while he bumbles about, willing to help with chores but entranced with the city and its inhabitants. His transition from country bumpkin to urban worker is not fast enough for his mother, who sends Manuel off to work in his uncle's shoe shop.

Among his street-wise cousins, Manuel is an innocent who remains uninterested in fighting, scheming, and whoring. When Leandro kills his girlfriend in a jealous rage, then commits suicide, the shoe shop closes.

The cousins invite Manuel to go to Italy with them to look for work, but he loves Justa, a pretty girl he met at the *pensión*, and prefers to stay in Madrid. He finds jobs, first at a bakery and, later, at a print shop, and is badly exploited at both. His boss at the bakery is a drunk who relaxes at the end of a long day by reclining with his bottle and striking with a whip the nude pinup on his wall. He tells Manuel that he, too, began by coming from his village to Madrid to look for work.

Not only is Manuel's economic world closed to opportunity; he also encounters a rigid social hierarchy as soon as he arrives at the *pensión*. He falls in love with Justa and continues to see her, promising that he will not always work at the shoe shop. Justa remains friendly, almost teasing him, and his longing for her keeps his ambition alive. But one day Manuel sees her at a café with a prosperous-looking businessman. He joins them, showing her the galleys from the print shop as evidence of his successful climb in the world. But his behavior and dress are so inferior to those of her middle-class companion that she laughs at him and says, distantly, "Come another day, Manuel."

Finally disillusioned with Justa, Manuel has a few drinks, loses the galley proofs that Tomás the printer had entrusted to him, and stumbles home to fall asleep on the floor. A shot of the iron window bars shadowing his inert form is a visual reminder that he is a prisoner of a relentlessly immobile society. As if to reinforce the full dimensions of this social theme, the director follows Justa's rebuff with a scene of the death of Manuel's mother. He goes to the *pensión* to pick up her things. Her tiny room is empty, her personal belongings rolled up in a blanket. The camera closes in on her worn black boots sitting atop the roll. Nearby perch two kittens who stare wide-eyed at the camera. Like Manuel, they are innocents pathetically unaware of the destructive world they inhabit.

From this point in the narrative, Manuel's fortunes decline steadily. With Justa and his mother now gone, Manuel loses his job at the print shop and returns to the only people he knows, his thieving cousins. They include him in their raids, but among them he is an outsider. Here, however, the only worthwhile event of his life occurs when his cousin Vidal's mistress, Rosa, falls in love with him.

Drawn to his innocence and respect for women, which make Manuel unique in his world, Rosa makes love to the young failure while a fight brews outside. Manuel hears Vidal calling her and goes out, only to be drawn into a fight with El Bizco. Rosa runs to Manuel and throws herself on him to protect him. This display of passion infuriates Vidal, who drags her away screaming. El Bizco falls on his own knife and dies. The others flee, leaving Manuel alone to await the guards who will come to arrest him for killing a man he did not harm. Exhausted, his hand bleeding, Manuel sits down and cries, unable to avoid the injustice that will now be added to the cruelty and hopelessness the world has handed him so far.

*La busca,* loosely based on the novel of the same name by Pío Baroja, is a study in social Darwinism. Rather than rendering faithfully one specific novel, the film reflects the pessimism of all Baroja's works. The conditions in which Manuel lives are so dismal and so far beyond being altered by individual effort that, as the documentary introduction implies, only change on a wide scale will improve the lives of unskilled laborers such as Manuel.

When *La busca* was viewed at Cannes, it was considered by foreign critics to lack a contemporary film style.[3] Yet it is a period piece, set in the first decade of the twentieth century. Its cinematography, simple and direct, recalls that of *Los olvidados,* with which it shares many parallels. Like Buñuel, director Angelino Fons begins *La busca* with a documentary tone. Like Buñuel, he is content to allow his social statement to prevail without cinematic cosmetics of any sort. The result is one of the most powerful dramatic narratives of Spanish cinema.

Jaime Camino's *Mañana será otro día* (*Tomorrow's Another Day*) (1966) is a less pessimistic updating of the theme of unemployment. Nowhere near the artistic power of *La busca, Mañana será otro día* is more picaresque than neorealist and makes its comments with humor and irony. The basic lines of the story have been modernized so that the protagonists are two unmarried lovers who steal a car and drive across the *meseta,* the arid Spanish plain that extends from Madrid almost to Barcelona, to seek their fortune in Spain's industrial capital. Neither owns anything except an attractive physical appearance, which they try to market in Barcelona's movie and television industries.

*Mañana será otro día* presents a female protagonist who conflicts with traditional Spanish attitudes toward women. Lisa rejects the image of women forged by the Franco myth because she is single, has no children, and asserts her independence. When she and Paco check into a hotel, the clerk insists that, since they are not married, they cannot stay. She becomes furious, insists that they are married, and threatens to call the police, at which the frightened room clerk relents. Like many unemployed young women, Lisa resorts to prostitution on occasion. For the most part, however, she remains faithful to Paco and is able to find work making TV advertisements and modeling haute couture fashions.

In his search for employment Paco turns up a gallery of devious characters. He becomes a secretary for a rich industrialist who also deals in stolen art and unscrupulous real-estate transfers. One afternoon Paco spots his boss disguised as a cleric trying to evade the police. As the boss enters the public baths, Paco quickly steals his car and drives away with Lisa to nearby Torremolinos, singing "Mañana será otro día," an upbeat song accompanied by the sound of castanets.

As an anthology of unemployment problems in Spain, *Mañana será otro día* presents corruption, prostitution, and car theft as survival techniques in a country whose outmoded morality and inadequate educational system create a population unprepared to compete efficiently in modern job markets. Neither Paco nor Lisa has any marketable intellectual skills, so that exploitation of their bodies is immediate and inevitable. They find better educated and more competent foreigners holding jobs in their own country that should be open to them but for which they are unprepared. "Estas chicas extranjeras" (These foreign girls), moans Lisa, eying her competition. Finally, the ironic title and the clicking castanets of the final scene underline the ancient Spanish attitude toward work, which is to put it off as long as possible. Aimed at a popular audience in the style of light comic farce, *Mañana será otro día* is a critique of Spanish society as well as a comment about those who enter the Spanish job market without success.

## Directors of the 1970's

With the exception of Carlos Saura, Manuel Summers is one of the few directors who, during the *franquista* period, was able to make films continuously and thus produce a body of work that can be associated with an identifiable style. Summers follows in the popular manner of Berlanga with lighthearted satire and burlesque of social problems. And Berlanga must recognize himself as Summers's predecessor. Just as Buñuel acted in a small role in Saura's *Llanto por un bandido*, Berlanga can be seen playing a policeman in Summers's *¿Porqué te engaña tu marido?* Like Berlanga, Summers enjoys shooting movies full of domestic turbulence, marital disputes, and frustrated married males whose sexual fantasies far outreach the confines of conventional morality.

Children are of special interest to Summers. Like Truffaut, he seems to have a talent for revealing children as small beings inhabiting a world parallel to, dependent upon, but entirely distinct from that of adults. It is from the child's ingenuous but honest vantage point that Summers, while not threatening the adult world, is able to make it appear quaint and ridiculous. The title of what is still his best film, *Adiós, cigüeña, adiós* (*Goodbye Stork*) (1970), is taken from the folk attitudes that modern adults still hold toward the education of their children about sex.

These attitudes are ridiculed in the opening frames of the film by juxtaposition of anatomical drawings of a pregnant female's abdomen with shots of a stork delivering a baby. Which of these images prevails in the classroom to educate children? The camera cuts to a classroom. A mounted stork stands before a blackboard drawing of the Virgin Mary. The class visits the Prado museum, where Goya's *Maja desnuda* and Rubens's fleshy nudes offer the children their first and only opportunity to observe human anatomy.

Two of the classmates—Paloma, thirteen, and Arturo, fifteen—are in love. They share the attention and affection they do not get from their parents. Paloma lives with her grandmother while her father promotes Japanese watches in Barcelona. He passes by home occasionally and directs Paloma to prepare his bath. Arturo's parents are equally noncommunicative. At school the nuns are busily rehearsing students for the Christmas play, in which Paloma plays the Virgin. Arturo, wearing a pair of wings, dangles from the ceiling by a rope in his role as an angel.

Expected sources of information about sex—parents and teachers—are found to be evasive, preoccupied, or, in the case of Arturo's father, openly hostile. So when Paloma becomes pregnant, their group of friends, ranging in age from eight to fifteen, must rely upon their own limited knowledge. Even Arturo's efforts to make the couple respectable fail. His father explodes with anger when Arturo states that he wants to get married. The priest tells him he's too young. He thinks of going to India, where he learns marriage is legal at age twelve, but the travel agent demands a passport, for which parental approval is required. Having heard that babies born out of wedlock are stupid or take years to be born, the group of kids insists upon a wedding ceremony. Bobbing about in two boats on the Retiro Park Lagoon, they pronounce Arturo and Paloma man and wife and prepare to deliver the baby themselves.

Directed by one of the older girls, Marmen, who can read and organize well, the group of kids prepares a room for Paloma in an attic. Paloma, having told her grandmother that she will be away doing "social service," is well cared for by the group. They sell their treasures to buy medical texts on childbirth. Hanging out at the prenatal clinic after school, they watch procedures and listen to the clients' conversations. The children soon consider the baby to be of collective parentage and draw lots to decide its name: Paloma, if a girl; Draculín (Little Dracula), if a boy.

When Paloma begins labor, the attic becomes very tense. Some of the younger children, watching her suffer, decide that "having a baby is not worth it"; others think she is dying. The division of workers in the attic is opposite from that in hospital delivery rooms, where the only females are sometimes a nurse and sometimes the newborn and its mother.

In the attic, the girls request the boys to wait outside, but they are terrified. As labor continues, someone describes "a dilation of three pesetas." When the baby appears they think it is dead and call in Arturo. Finally it cries and the kids cheer, "El niño, boom, boom, ba." Across the last frame flies the ironic image of the stork. The kids will be able to tell some surprised adults their own version of the stork story in which a stork brings a baby to a group of young children. *Adiós, cigüeña, adiós* makes some honest comparisons between child and adult behavior in which maturity lies altogether with the children.

Throughout the *franquista* period historical extravaganzas were used by both the establishment and the opposition to manipulate public sentiment. If the promilitary, patriotic right wing glorifies the family, sacrifice, and heroism in battle, the opposition also attempts to impress its values by analogy. Pedro Olea achieves special success in the historical genre with two period films. The first, *Tormento* (1974), revives the nineteenth century and is based on a novel of the same name by Spain's great realist writer Benito Pérez Galdós.

*Tormento* is an excellent example of how use of color film often detracts from narrative strength by becoming spectacular and drawing attention away from the action. This is what happens from the beginning of *Tormento*, which, if made in black and white, might have equaled *La busca*. But its color is too luscious to visually convey hard times as anything but visual spectacle. Even the opening presentation of titles is sumptuous: blood-red titles on a background of what resemble Goya prints. Olea, repeating Fons's use of the dissolve to turn history into fiction, focuses on Goya's print to begin the action. But the change from black and white to color film explodes the emotional tone from deprivation into visual feast.

Although *Tormento's* visual beauty undermines its critical force, character development and dialogue remain instruments of social analysis. These are especially effective in the hands of a superb cast. Conchita Velasco plays Rosario, the domineering, cruel, and materialistic wife of a provincial lawyer. She and her husband are visited by don Agustín, played by Francisco Rabal. He is an *indio,* a Spaniard brought up in Mexico who returns to Spain to enjoy the wealth he made abroad. Complicating the narrative is Amparo, a young woman whose parents died and left her and her sister as children in the care of Rosario. Amparo, without status or fortune of her own, serves in the household as maid. Rosario plans to banish her to a convent as soon as possible, but she is not quick enough. Before Rosario can put the young woman away in a convent, Agustín arrives bearing gifts for everyone and falls in love with Amparo. Agustín's love for Amparo and his attempt to win her in spite of her past provide the basic plot around which the theme of class hatred looms as central. Amparo, played with admirable control by Ana Belén, has the impassive face of the victim of circumstances who must hide her emotions. While reading in shadowed light she resembles the waxen faces in the paintings of Georges de la Tour, but her restraint belies considerable passion. As an orphan, she fell under the influence of Pedro and became his mistress. Although her relations with him have long ceased, Amparo is still harassed by Pedro, who is now a drop-out priest.

Amparo makes the generous but mistaken move of going to visit Pedro one last time before he leaves, as he has begged her to do. It is her misfortune that doña Marcelina, whose face incarnates every detail of malicious gossip in the guise of charity, chooses this moment to visit Pedro's mother, who is ill. Doña Marcelina discovers Amparo's presence and wastes no time in relaying this delicious morsel of news to Rosario. The camera focuses on Rosario the next morning, smiling with all the refined luxury of which a puritan is capable. When Amparo appears, Rosario, a delicate lilt in her voice, sinks her verbal dagger into Amparo with consummate ecstasy: "There has been a change of plans." Conchita Velasco, a venomous little smile on her lips, delivers this devastating line with uncanny timing and simplicity.

Don Agustín (Francisco Rabal), who had bought a house and expected to live a respectable life in the town with his loving wife, Amparo, is annoyed at having his virginal image of her destroyed and he smashes the silver hand-mirror he had initialed for her. This dream gone, he plans to leave for Paris and pays her a farewell visit. She is recuperating well from attempted suicide and, somewhat belatedly, tells him the story of her past. It is sordid and he prefers not to hear it, but she is determined that he fully understand her. It is a woman's story of poverty, dependence, and exploitation, none of which he has apparently experienced firsthand.

The final scene is a triumph of love over class hatred. Don Agustín boards the train for Paris and waves farewell to Rosario and her family, who stand on the platform waving fondly. They see that Agustín turns to someone in the train compartment. The camera focuses on Rosario's smile as it freezes. In unison with the train as it puffs out of the station, the infuriated Rosario whispers, "Puta, puta, puta" (Bitch, bitch, bitch). Her visions of respectability, which served her interests and power so well, disappear with the train. Don Agustín, who needs love, has decided that it does not necessarily have to be packaged in the bonds of morality established by Rosario and the society she represents. If the Spanish bourgeoisie refuse to accept Amparo as his wife, she can be his mistress in Paris. As for Amparo, it is her turn to smile. She waves as the train pulls her mercifully from the clutches of Rosario, who only now catches a glimpse of her former maid as she escapes provincial Spanish social rigidity.

In *Pim, pam, pum, ¡fuego!* (1975), one of the most courageous films of the *franquista* period, Olea turns from the nineteenth century to the 1940s, the early post–Civil War period. Bread lines and housing shortages are seen as part of daily life, not just one-moment clips from a faded documentary. In an introductory scene on a train, Paquita, a dancer, meets Luis, the maquis (unrepatriated Republican soldier). She agrees to hide Luis in her apartment until he can obtain documents with which to escape across the border into France. The versatile Conchita Velasco, who excelled as the shrewish Rosario in *Tormento,* is entirely convincing as the outgoing but exploited Paquita of *Pim, pam, pum, ¡fuego!*

The development of this ominous narrative is interrupted by scenes of nightclub acts in which Paquita sings songs popular in the 1940s. Paquita auditions in front of aging playboys, who eye her legs without hearing her songs. Julio helps her get a job in a dance hall where customers come to escape from the miseries of postwar life. Songs like "California" are performed by chorus girls dressed in boots and cowboy hats. Such festivity contrasts sharply with the conditions of life in Madrid.

The central character is Julio, a blackmarketeer who cruelly manipulates the lives of others. The character of Julio is not ambiguous: he is a villain whose motives are ulterior. The film probably passed censorship because Julio's political position is left undefined so that his actions may be interpreted as resulting from jealousy as well as from loyalty to the *franquista* cause.

Julio befriends Paquita and presents her with gifts of food and other scarce items. Although she has fallen in love with Luis, Paquita becomes Julio's mistress in return for a new apartment for her and her aged invalid father. On moving day, Luis makes the move to the new apartment hiding in a wardrobe which is loaded onto the back of a truck. When, inevitably, Julio discovers Luis's presence, Paquita tells him everything about Luis except for the fact that she loves him. She presents him to Julio as her cousin.

The character of Julio is enacted by one of Spain's finest actors, Fernando Fernán Gómez, whose acting abilities range from the laconic comedy of Walter Matthau roles, to the troubled priest in *Balarrasa,* to complex and deceptive villains such as the refined murderer in *Pim, pam, pum, ¡fuego!* Fernán Gómez ably portrays the multiple stages of jealousy, appearing generous at first while knowing Paquita does not love him, then concealing anger at her story about her "cousin." Julio enjoys slowly humiliating Paquita and insulting her in public before driving her out to a lonely road. He shows her a newspaper announcement of the death of a maquis killed while attempting escape across the border. Julio's last words to Paquita confirm her suspicion that he obtained Luis's documents and paid to have him shot.

Then with the cool detachment of a professional killer, Julio takes out his pistol, puts it against Paquita's head, and pulls the trigger. He pushes her body out the car door, turns the car around, and drives at a normal speed back down the highway. The deliberate pace of this scene allows the spectator to absorb the surprisingly brutal ending and realize the horrible irony of the title of the film, which can be translated as "Just Like That, Bang."

As with *Tormento,* Pedro Olea's voluptuous use of color film distracts from the recreation of an era of hard times. The interior of the train, for example, is furnished in the style of the past, but the two radiant characters, Luis and Paquita, do not seem to suffer from postwar hunger or neglect. The other train passengers are, of course, dressed in dull garb but are not ravaged by war. Other crowd scenes and street shots also fail to render deprivation very convincingly. So *Pim, pam, pum, ¡fuego!* will be remembered, as is *Tormento,* for its dramatic characterizations that personify the manipulation and brutality encouraged by postwar scarcity.

The scriptwriters of Ricardo Franco's *Pascual Duarte* (1976) agree that Camilo José Cela's novel by the same name, one of the monuments of twentieth-century Spanish fiction, served them not as a model they tried to follow faithfully but rather as a point of departure.[4] Through distancing and spare use of historical details their film achieves a dimension, entirely lacking in the novel, which converts fiction into ethnographic film. For, in describing Pascual's world visually, Ricardo Franco suggests that his protagonist inhabits an early culture closer to the Third World than to the postindustrial West.

Blood-red titles on black background accompany intensely repetitive and ominous guitar music. Written by one of Spain's best young composers, Luis de Pablo, the sharp, nervous notes are the only sound in the long introductory sequence. Against this phonic background the camera focuses on Extremadura, one of Spain's poorest provinces: yellow, barren farm land, no vegetation, a section plowed in furrows, an endless horizon. In the distance the camera focuses on three figures who seem lost together in this landscape—two guards with rifles and their handcuffed prisoner. A close shot shows handcuffed wrists trying to light a cigarette. This desolate corner of the planet is silent. As yet, no dialogue intrudes. An army truck stops, picks up the three men, and drives off.

A flashback narrates the prisoner's story. In a dark schoolroom a boy of about seven is learning to read by reciting aloud from the Bible the story of Isaac and Abraham—an early lesson in slaughter and sacrifice. Outside some of the boy's playmates wave, inviting him to join them, which he does without the old schoolmaster understanding what happened to the reader. The boy, Pascual, and his friends run across the open fields until they find a tree to climb. In the tree they discover a bird's nest where fledglings, like themselves, have begun life hungry.

Poverty is a fundamental condition of life in this remote Spanish province. Franco's army has trucks, while the peasants walk or ride mules. The mayor lives in a spacious house in the village, while peasants live in ill-lit hovels in the countryside. In addition to abysmal poverty, monstrous human ignorance keeps the peasants prisoners of their hostile, drought-stricken province. Pascual's father can barely read newspaper headlines. He frequently gets drunk. When he staggers into the hovel to

Rosario (Diana Pérez de Guzmán) comforts Pascual (José Luis Gómez) in Ricardo Franco's *Pascual Duarte* (1975).

abuse Pascual's mother, she locks "ese Portugués de mierda" (that filthy Portuguese) in the pig barn until he sobers up.

As might be expected in this primitive world, love and rape are almost indistinguishable, the only difference being that when Pascual (José Luis Gómez) hits Lola in the face, knocks her down, and rapes her, she marries him instead of trying to escape. Three objects elicit sporadic displays of tenderness from Pascual: his dog, whom he pets when hunting, then slaughters with his shotgun for no apparent reason; his gun, which he caresses in cleaning as Saura's hunters caressed theirs in *La caza;* and his sister Rosario, whom he nurses devotedly through an illness. When Rosario recovers and packs her bag to return to her husband, Eusabio, Pascual first tells her not to go. He holds a grudge against Eusabio, who teased him once about his love for Rosario. She tells Pascual she cannot stay and continues packing. Without a word Pascual picks up his shotgun, marches outside, and blows Eusabio to shreds as he had his dog—at point-blank range.

The stunned viewer quickly searching for explanations for the murderous behavior first considers insanity. Ricardo Franco, however, as did Miguel Picazo in *La tía Tula* a decade before, rejects madness and instead offers images suggesting cultural causes for apparently irrational action.

The ominous, silent presence of army trucks passing back and forth; the enormous implicit advantage of army transportation over peasants on foot or mules; groups of unemployed men who quarrel in the streets and are later seen occupying the jail cells—all hint at a power structure in which peasants maintain a vastly inferior status.

Details of rural community life are offered in shots of the mayor and other villagers voting. That night, people cluster around an old box radio and listen to the announcer exulting, "¡Viva la República!" a cry which alludes to the fact that the year is 1931, when Spain freely elected a short-lived democratic government. But the people of this region are silent and share only scraps of dialogue. Their ignorance has left them without a voice, unable to make their needs known or express themselves except in crude monosyllables or by words provided them by public scribes. Mute and isolated, with the unexplained presence of force as their only model of behavior, these Spanish peasants can only express their frustrations by violent rather than productive means. For them there exists no pattern of productive life.

Pascual, of course, spends time in jail for murder. When he leaves jail he ironically enters a more solitary world than the one he had known in confinement. Other freed prisoners are welcomed upon release by relatives. No one waits for Pascual. Since Lola's death, which Pascual mourned by stabbing a mule to death, there is no one who cares about him. He returns to an empty house. When his mother arrives they neither speak nor touch. He is an outcast. Looking for the mayor's help in finding work, Pascual hears only that things are bad for everyone. Now an ex-convict, the hopeless man gets no encouragement from the mayor, his last source for earning his livelihood.

It is within this context of solitude, abandonment, implicit inferiority, and repression that Pascual, sitting one night cleaning his gun, suddenly and deliberately pulls back the latches on its double barrels, leans back in his chair, and fires at his mother as he sits across the table from her. So apparently gratuitous, this action is the last in a long-established pattern of violence and ignorance amid a total lack of any opportunity for a better life. Like the other killings he has committed, Pascual murders his mother without speaking a word, in silent, deadly frustration.

Only in the agony of death does Pascual emit any sound—a loud excruciating cry of horror. The final scene of Pascual's being dragged to his execution ends with a close freeze shot of the Spanish style of executing prisoners. Garroting, used until only a few decades ago in Spain, is carried out by slowly tightening an iron collar around the prisoner's neck. Ricardo Franco's close look at the medieval form of execution is both a metaphor for a slowly asphyxiating, repressive culture as well as for stark reality in Spain.

Pascual dies by garrote in a Spanish prison in Ricardo Franco's *Pascual Duarte* (1975).

*Pascual Duarte* is exceeded in its brutality only by José Luis Borau's *Furtivos* (*Poachers*) (1975), a film Peruvian writer Mario Vargas Llosa calls "One of the cruelest stories in Spanish cinema."[5] The action of *Furtivos* is set in the opulent natural beauty of northern Spain near Santander. It is based on actual events that took place in the village of Bosque del Saja. A family of *furtivos*, Angel and his mother, Martina, lives near a small village in spectacular woodland scenery. The autumn air is crisp, weeds and leaves redden in the frosty air. The ambulance siren of the opening scene in the village, however, is an immediate clue that things are not as peaceful as they seem.

As in *Pascual Duarte*, the presence of military force is a silent, intimidating commonplace. From a quick shot of a group of local militia, the camera cuts to a young man buying wire and cartridges in a shop. It is Angel, purchasing the tools of his trade for the careful and continuous slaughter of wild animals that, like he, inhabit the woods near the village. Angel leaves the shop and sits on a bench to eat his lunch. A girl on the opposite bench stares at him, waggles her open legs, and moves to sit by him. They bite into his sausage sandwich and she invites him to "buy her something." He buys her a dress which she tries on behind a doorway.

The eroticism of their encounter contrasts with a return to the woods.

The camera closes in on the scrawny, aging face of Martina, Angel's mother. The role is enacted by Lola Gaos, who gained international fame as the patient Saturna in Buñuel's *Tristana*. In *Furtivos* she plays the cunning, long-suffering, incestuous mother of the silent and murderous Angel. Ovidi Montllor portrays the cunning, vulnerable, and finally cruel Angel with great restraint.

Martina appears immediately to be a sympathetic character as she strolls through the woods snapping the steel-jawed traps Angel has carefully concealed in the leaves. An early harbinger of her own fate is the wolf Martina discovers caught in one of the traps. She tries to end its agony by cleaving it with an ax and dragging the screaming beast to a cave where she leaves it to die. Part of the impact of this scene, as Vargas Llosa points out, is that the image of the wolf's death is not only symbolic but is a powerful image by itself.[6]

Angel returns late with his new girl, Milagros. Martina, out of sympathy for a suffering beast, had dragged the maddened wolf to a cave. Now Angel, with no such compassion, drags the sleeping Martina from her bed, kicks her out of the room, and installs himself and Milagros in the bed. Martina, desperate with fury, swigs from her ever-present wine bottle, takes an ax, and returns to kill the agonizing wolf, thus venting her own anger but foreshadowing her own fate. For the wolf is, like Martina, female. Angel demands a tidy sum for the pelt when he sells it in town, because, he claims, "the female wolves are the most dangerous." The fur dealer pays the price but warns Angel not to expect any more, or "I'll turn you in for poaching."

Despite Milagros's shady past as a reformatory escapee, Angel marries her while knowing that she loves a local tough, El Cuqui. She later confesses to El Cuqui that she married Angel to avoid being sent back to the reformatory. But Martina does not share her son's affection for the young woman. She submits to having Milagros in the household; but, as the camera closes in on her bone-tired eyes and thin, tight-set mouth, she entertains murderous thoughts about Milagros as they dig truffles together in the woods. An additional character completing this vicious group is the provincial governor, who is also Martina's son.

Older and brighter than the silent Angel, the governor, in his position of political power, represents law and order. He regularly takes his friends to stay at Martina's and hunt in the woods. One day Angel kills the beautiful black stag the governor himself had hoped to bag as a trophy. We see the splendid animal dying a slow and tortured death. The governor is furious, but his only recourse is to require Angel to register for a permit to bear arms, thus legalizing his slaughter of animals. The governor then becomes an accomplice to the slaughter, for he, too, enjoys lying in wait for and killing wild animals. Angel files for the permit and begs the governor to look for Milagros. Angel begins to hunt for and eventually finds El Cuqui. Softened when Milagros promises to stay with him, Angel lets his rival go, telling El Cuqui only that Milagros doesn't love him.

Martina, however, can hardly contain her glee that Milagros has departed. She begins to spoil Angel, treating him like a lover, thus revealing the incestuous bonds which have distorted the relationship between her and her younger son. When he pushes her away and goes upstairs, the camera frames her face in the square stairwell from above as she taunts, "She didn't love you. She only came to await her boyfriend." Her relief is Angel's bitter pain. Angel goes to the village and sits on the bench where he first met Milagros. Suddenly he looks up and sees El Cuqui lurking between two parked buses. "Tell Milagros I'm looking for her," whispers the outlaw and runs off.

Angel now assumes that, since Milagros is not with her outlaw lover, Martina has killed her. We have watched Martina enjoying thoughts of ridding herself of the intruder; however, this haggard and harassed woman seems hardly capable of carrying them out. As Buñuel's police chief tells Archibaldo de la Cruz, "Who hasn't thought of murder at one time or another?" Postwar Spanish cinema, however (*La caza, Pim, pam, pum, ¡fuego!, Pascual Duarte*), testifies that humans are often engaged in hunting down other creatures, or each other, so that they may be loosely divided into two classes—hunter and prey. Suddenly, Martina, from this point in *Furtivos,* becomes the prey.

When Angel returns from town she is plucking a chicken she plans to cook. He stares at her, telling her that tomorrow they must go to church. The next day he chats at length with the priest as he helps him don his cassock. After the fearful Martina has gone to confession, Angel marches her through the snow, holding his shotgun. When he steps back a few steps, the terrified Martina asks, "What will you do to me?" Still, as if admitting guilt, she makes no attempt to protest. "You know," shouts Angel as he pulls the trigger of his shotgun. As calmly as he had shot the governor's black stag—deliberately and without remorse—Angel walks home, gets a bottle of wine, and begins once more going through the small box containing Milagros's trinkets.

*Furtivos* suffers from an excessively elliptical treatment of its narrative. In films dealing with mystery and the impossibility of knowing truth, ambiguity, as in *Viridiana,* enriches by offering various possibilities. But Borau is not a philosopher, and the film that he begins as a strong political statement soon turns into a detective story. His first effort at making a long-suffering female into a killer was in *El crimen de doble filo* (1964), a well-constructed murder and suspense thriller. Ten years later in *Furtivos* he attempts to reach beyond escapism, still depending on the detective genre for its formal structure.

*Pascual Duarte* and *Furtivos,* culminating nearly forty years of Spanish cinema, are two of the best films of the entire *franquista* period. They share enough important parallels that further insight into their meaning may be gained by brief comparative analysis: themes of exploitation, ignorance, and violence are central to each of these films. Their provincial protagonists, educated briefly if at all, do not function as members of a social group but keep to themselves and act alone. These lone killers, however, live within the context of violence. Armed guards or militia in their villages are a constant threat, echoed in widespread personal use of arms. In both films, the protagonists use guns for the slaughter of animals and humans. Thus the carrying of weapons seems to be a social pattern with legal sanction for both public and private use.

Hunting, a vital activity in tribal societies, retains only ritual function in contemporary life. As a theme in these two films, hunting signifies not only the tribal nature of life in isolated provinces, but by extension in Franco's Spain. It offers a simple solution to complex human problems. The repressed Pascual's anger lies so deep he vents his frustration on defenseless substitutes for his real victims, such as his hunting dog, which he kills with his shotgun without apparent motive. In *Furtivos* as well hunting and its illegal variant, poaching, are presented as closely related vestiges of a long-outmoded way of provincial life.

That death is a frequent theme in films of a postwar era is not surprising. But it is a curious coincidence that the protagonists of two major films of the 1970s resort to matricide. The figure of the mother has never been very positive in Spanish theater, if portrayed at all. From Calderón's "terrible mother" of the seventeenth century to Galdós's doña Perfecta of the nineteenth century and Lorca's Bernarda Alba of the twentieth, mothers are frequently depicted as villains in Spanish theater and fiction. In these two Spanish films, the cruel mothers are products of a society which is itself seen as corrupt. The incestuous Martina and the unforgiving mother of Pascual are murdered without the slightest sense of remorse, a fact that suggests that they are killed for reasons much more complex than simple vengeance.

The motif of matricide, executed in a calculated and calm manner, points to a kind of anthropology of Spanish culture elaborated by Ricardo Franco and José Luis Borau. *Pascual Duarte* and *Furtivos* seem to somehow equate the mother figure with Franco's Spain, a motherland now corrupt and cruel. On a metaphorical level, then, these two sons, Pascual and Angel, nurtured in corruption, punish the parent who has sinned against them with almost tribal violence. By suggesting that Franco's Spain has become as violent as some tribal groups, Ricardo Franco and Borau design identical analogies for the antiquated, marginal position of Franco's Spain in the modern world.

There are important differences between the two films: the remote settings in *Pascual Duarte* are harsh and barren, while in *Furtivos* the woods are splendid. The pace of the action, the interplay between plot and subplot in *Furtivos* sustain suspense as in a detective thriller, while *Pascual Duarte* is tedious with long periods of silence. The light and colors of the northern province are rich, often muted or darkening, contrasting with the glaring sunlight and empty geometry of plowed and unplowed fields in *Pascual Duarte*. Yet similar themes of cruelty and ignorance as well as identical motifs of animal slaughter and matricide signify that, from the northern woods to the plains of Extremadura, that is, from one end of Spain to another, the *franquista* period was one of unremitting if often clandestine violence.

I have left until last discussion of one of the most highly acclaimed films in the history of Spanish cinema, *El espíritu de la colmena (Spirit of the Beehive),* which has been haunting audiences both in Spain and abroad since it premiered in Madrid in October 1973. If Saura portrays postwar Spain with images of dismemberment and Ricardo Franco and Borau equate national violence with matricide, young Victor Erice, in search of new myths, turns to those of horror film to caricature his country as Frankenstein, a monster that has lost its memory.

Ana, protagonist of *Espíritu,* lives with her sister, Isabel, and their parents in a remote Castilian village, Hoyuelos. Spain in microcosm, Hoyuelos in 1941 seems to exist at the edge of the civilized world, connected to it only by a train. The sound track of the opening scenes underscores the isolation of the village with sounds of blowing wind and the melancholy whistle of the train as it passes through the village.

Ana, six, with Isabel, nine, goes to see James Whales's *Dr. Frankenstein.* She is deeply moved by the dual character of the monster. In bed at night, the sisters whisper about the movie. Ana asks Isabel why the monster kills the little girl and why he, too, is killed. Isabel, who knows these things, reassures her that Frankenstein is not dead. She tells Ana that Frankenstein is a spirit, that she herself has seen him and that "si eres su amigo, puedes hablar con él cuando quieras . . . Cierras los ojos y le llamas . . . 'Soy Ana, soy Ana'" (If you're his friend, you can talk to him whenever you want . . . You close your eyes and call him . . . 'I'm Ana, I'm Ana').[7]

The monster is just one of the mysteries of *Espíritu.* Teresa, the girls' mother, writes letters to an unknown person whom critics have identified variously as a lover or a lost child.[8] Fernando, her husband, is a beekeeper. Of their life before the Civil War we know only that it was better than their present one. Their only remaining vestige of better days is a photograph shown briefly on screen of Fernando and other students with

Ana Torrent watches *Frankenstein* in Victor Erice's *El espíritu de la colmena* (1974).

their professor, Miguel de Unamuno, the renowned philosopher who died on the eve of the conflict in 1936. The photo recalls the contrast between the intellectual conviviality of prewar life and the emptiness of the postwar years.

The house in which the family lives almost qualifies as the typical haunted house of horror film. It is large, empty, and, since the family has no electricity, dimly lit. The children run through a long hall upstairs, the doorways of each successive empty room framing their small forms until they appear to be swallowed down the corridor. The windows of the house are glass with small hexagonal panes, an image that equates the monotonous life of its inhabitants with that of the bees in Fernando's hives. Supporting this visual clue is the loud buzzing of the bees on the sound track. The color also contributes to the hive metaphor. Gifted cinematographer Luis Cuadrado shot the interior scenes through a yellow filter, thus creating the yellowed, antique look of the family home.

The dim, medieval gloom of the interior of the house is broken by the brilliant sunlight on the barren fields. Washed-out lighting emphasizes the harsh, empty, shadowless plain. The two sisters wander about in this stark landscape, waiting for the train to pass. Ana listens for its rumble

Isabel whispers to Ana during the movie in Erice's *El espíritu de la colmena* (1974).

with an ear on the tracks. They find an abandoned farm house with a well. Looking for Frankenstein, Ana calls into the well. As if following her voice, the camera peers down into the impenetrable darkness. Like the other sources of knowledge in this film—parents, friends, the outside world—the well reveals nothing.

One day Ana returns alone to the abandoned house and discovers there a wounded man sitting on the floor. His head is bandaged and he has a broken leg. The man hears Ana approach and draws his pistol. Seeing the child he hides the pistol and accepts an apple she offers him from her lunchbox. Ana, who believes the man to be Frankenstein, brings him things he may need from her home—bread, her father's shoes, and his jacket.

Ana's acceptance of Frankenstein as a friendly fellow is not without its visual justification. There is another character, also in physical disarray, that Ana sees every day in her school room. It is don José, with whose cardboard body fragments the children learn anatomy. "A ver, Ana, ¿qué más falta a don José?" (Let's see, Ana. What else does José lack?), asks the teacher, doña Lucía. Ana walks up to don José and places a pair of eyes where they should be in the same way she fearlessly approaches the

Ana (*standing*) and Isabel wait for the train in Erice's *El espíritu de la colmena* (1974).

wounded soldier with bandaged head and gives him an apple, believing him to be the friendly monster. Like don José, the monster is composed of add-on parts. As a metaphor for Spain, Frankenstein is a ghoulish collage, a monstrous figure constructed by a sinister creator whose name sounds very much like "Franco."

For the villagers, the wounded man is not Frankenstein but a maquis, of whom there were over fifty thousand at the close of the Civil War. To them he is a criminal and they kill him. Shots ring out abruptly in the night. The next morning the cadaver of the man Ana thought was Frankenstein lies on a slab in the theater, emphasizing that her Frankenstein is dead. The police have called in Fernando, since his pocket-watch was found in the dead man's jacket pocket. The puzzled Fernando goes home to breakfast with his family. He pulls out his pocket watch and looks at Ana, who stares at it, jumps up from the table, and runs to the abandoned house to find her friend has gone.

Ana runs off to find Frankenstein, looking like a little bird in her dark coat as she heads across the fields. A search is organized, but night falls without a trace of her. The camera discovers her sitting by a river peering at the reflection of the moon. Suddenly a dark form looms over her: Frankenstein. A close shot reveals Ana handing the monster a mushroom she has picked. A barking dog breaks the spell, announcing the approach of the search party, which finds her curled up in the hollow of an old tree.

In the final scene, Ana has recovered from her fright and from her vision of the monster. But she still feels a sense of loss. Unable to sleep one night, she climbs out of bed, opens the balcony window, and looks out at the moon. Recalling Isabel's instructions about talking to Frankenstein, Ana closes her eyes and, in a silent whisper, repeats, "Soy Ana" (I'm Ana). The only reply is the whistle of the train that passes through the village without stopping.

By referring to the horror myth of Frankenstein, Erice has discovered an uncannily accurate metaphor for Franco's Spain. As a character without a memory, Frankenstein has no moral sense and, thus, can behave kindly, then kill. As a mythical figure himself, Frankenstein aptly represents the end result of the Franco myth, for as Roland Barthes concludes, myth is characterized by the loss of historical perspective: "In it, things lose the memory that they were once made." [9]

The *estética franquista,* of which *Espíritu* is one of the most moving examples, may lack the power of other postwar cinema, such as Italian neorealism. With its abrupt cuts, obscure images and juxtapositions, unexplained actions, and incorporation of horror devices, the Spanish postwar film style borrows from surrealism and is often not easily accessible to unprepared viewers. For power of direct statement, however, these Spanish films substitute their ability to disturb and disquiet the mind of anyone whose national past also contains nightmares.

# 10. Transition: Dictatorship to Democracy, 1975–1980

Franco's death on November 20, 1975, brought hope that Spain, under the fascist fist for almost half the twentieth century, would now become a democracy. Franco designated as his successor Juan Carlos of Bourbon, grandson of the last king of Spain. Free elections were held for the first time in over forty years on June 15, 1977. In November 1977, censorship laws were revoked. The censorship board was instead charged with classifying films according to the age group for which they were most suitable. The classification "S" was supposedly reserved for the equivalent of the U.S. X-rated, or sexually explicit, film.

Cinema in Spain seemed free at last. Films never publicly released there could now be seen for the first time. Some, such as *Battleship Potemkin*, dated as far back as 1925. *Potemkin* and *Oktober* (1928) had been screened by film clubs but never released to the general public. New to Spain in 1975 were Chaplin's *The Great Dictator* (1940), Buñuel's *Viridiana* (1961), Costa-Gavra's *Z* (1968), and Joseph Losey's *Assassination of Trotsky* (1971). Also having their Spanish premier the year of Franco's death were films dealing with the Civil War, such as André Malraux's *Sierra de Teruel* (1938–39) and Alain Resnais' *La Guerre est finie* (1966).

Among these previously prohibited Civil War films were those by Spanish directors who alluded to the war in nostalgic compilations. One such film is Basilio Martín Patino's *Canciones para después de una guerra* (*Postwar Songs*), made in 1971 but not released until five years later. *Canciones* is a rambling memoir of the postwar era unified by a sound track of popular songs from the 1940s and 1950s. Awesome documentary footage of war damages is followed by views of Franco's victory march into Madrid, accompanied by the triumphal song "Aquí no pasarán" ("They Won't Get Past Here"). Bread lines, blackmarket buying and selling, and scenes of people digging out of rubble and ruined buildings, accompanied by the lilting voice of Imperio Argentina, characterize Spanish life in the 1940s.

The decade of the 1950s is heralded in *Canciones* by the arrival of Americans, from movie stars to military heroes. Quick shots of Ava Gardner flinging a rose into a bullring contrast with the more ominous presence of Evita Perón waving at huge crowds massed below Franco's balcony. Banners proclaiming loyalty to Franco carried by marchers at rallies are contradicted by newspaper clippings reporting terrorist bombings that punctuated the decade.

*Canciones* is an ironic juxtaposition of nostalgia with scenes betraying the realities of life under Franco. Insight into Spanish education is gained in scenes of young girls being taught washing, cleaning, sewing, and cooking while young men attend classes and begin careers. Public health consists of a priest blessing the wounds of hundreds of war casualties. Scenes of Spanish dances and bullfights accompany news of the atom bomb, suggesting Spain's continued isolation from the industrial/technological West.

Another such work is Patino's *Caudillo* (*Military Boss*) (1976), an ironic portrait compiled from footage in archives in London, Paris, and Lisbon. *Caudillo* attempts to explain Franco's rise by analogy with other dictators. Evidence of military support for a fascist leader in Spain is expressed by the infamous slogan "Viva la muerte" (Long live death) shouted by Millán Astray, one of Franco's loyal generals to the rural poor who hailed Franco's advance.

As in *Canciones,* information in *Caudillo* is conveyed by allusion and juxtaposition of images rather than by direct narrative. Documents included are shots of newspaper clippings reporting the murder of the poet García Lorca and graffiti referring to the "assassin of the Spanish people," as well as film footage from Franco's life. Songs of triumph, the dictator's dogmatic pronouncements, and florid, pious military rhetoric fill the sound track.

*Caudillo* also makes clear the radical difference between the styles of life of the two opposing sides. In towns and villages under Nationalist control, daily duties were carried out with military discipline and strict ritualistic patterns of behavior. Uniforms, parades, hierarchy, and the invisibility of the nonmilitary populace produce a stark contrast with Republican villages, where the populace mobilized for war with few authoritarian forms of behavior and a lack of structured discipline.

Patino's montage of images from Franco's career is not a history but a dialectic whose ironic dialogue and commentary convey revulsion and ridicule of his central figure.[1] "No persigo dar información, sólo doy sentimientos" (I do not pretend to inform, I only supply the sentiment), Patino admits.[2] The sentiment did not please Spanish officials who, even without official censorship, were able to prevent circulation of posters and other promotional material of *Caudillo* when it was presented at the

1976 Berlin Film Festival. Yet *Caudillo* continues the *estética franquista* in its oblique, indirect undermining of the Franco myth.

It became clear that until Spanish film archives are accessible to the public, directors would have to substitute compilations of their own making, such as Patino's two films, for actual newsreel footage. *Caudillo* and *Canciones* set a model for the first inquiries into the Civil War. Ironic use of filmed interviews forms the basis for other attempts to recapture the conflict, as in Jaime Camino's *La vieja memoria* (*The Long Memory*) and Jaime Chávarri's *El desencanto* (*Disillusion*), both shot in 1976.

*La vieja memoria* is a nearly three-hour series of interviews with important political figures who both supported and opposed the fascist rise. They include the famous Communist La Pasionaria (Dolores Ibarruri), Christian Social Democrat Gil Robles, former dictator Primo de Rivera, Falangist secretary-minister Raimundo Fernández Cuesta, Federica Montseny, José Luis Villalonga, Jaime Miravitelles, and many others. Their recollections of the Civil War serve as a kind of family photograph such as Saura uses to introduce his metaphorical films, but in *La vieja memoria* the persons interviewed speak of their roles in the conflict. Camino, who holds a law degree and has studied music, uses the sound track to dramatize the words of the speakers. The Falangist dictator Primo de Rivera is accompanied by Strauss's *Thus Spake Zarathustra*, which echoes the speaker's pomposity.

A similar effort to document the past is Jaime Chávarri's *El desencanto*, a series of interviews with members of the family of *franquista* poet Leopoldo Panero, who died in 1962. The family members talk openly before the camera about themselves and their long family history. The remarks of Panero's widow and children, like those of Pilar Franco in *Raza, el espíritu de Franco*, are more revealing than most fictional or historical accounts. "The Panero family," Chávarri remarked, "has not known what work is for four or five centuries."[3] Vicente Molina Foix compares this family portrait to another intimate look at an isolated, unaware, slightly grotesque family unit entitled *Gray Gardens*.[4]

These testimonials, in which interviews and film fragments are put to music in a way that seems to either confirm or incriminate them, culminate in Gonzálo Herralde's *Raza, el espíritu de Franco* (1977). Herralde makes no effort to analyze the dictator's career. His primary interest is not Franco but the manipulation of film for propaganda purposes. The director explains that his film "no es un ataque a la figura política de Franco . . . lo que pretende es desvelar la verdad oculta detrás de todo un aparato discursivo que Franco estableció" (is not an attack on the political figure of Franco . . . what is intended is to reveal the hidden truth behind a stylistic apparatus that Franco established).[5]

*Raza, el espíritu de Franco*, like *Caudillo*, is another important first step in the demystification of Franco. The director brings out the fact that Franco's novel, *Raza,* although published under a pseudonym, is still fictional biography. The 1941 film based on it allowed the dictator not only to tell his life story but to control the narration of events and his own personal image as the protagonist. The short, dark general is played by the tall, blonde Alfredo Mayo, the movie image of the fascist hero of the 1940s and 1950s. Ironically, in one of Herralde's interviews with Mayo, the actor confesses that he never understood the meaning of *raza hispánica,* a grandiose phrase Franco used to convey his own conception of the Civil War as a "crusade" against infidels.[6] The interviews with Mayo allow the viewer to separate fact from fantasy, to see clearly the enlargement of character by which Franco hoped to legitimate, if not make more palatable, his role as Spain's savior. Excerpts from the 1941 *Raza* are included, as well as interviews with the dictator's sister Pilar Franco. By confirming that events narrated in the novel actually occurred to her brother, she unwittingly provides evidence that the novel, and the film based on it, were indeed biographical, thus confirming Franco's design to imprint his own image into the fabric of Spanish history. Herralde's *Raza, el espíritu de Franco* accomplishes the crucial task of revealing to Spaniards the process by which the film version distorted history. Unfortunately, one of Spain's best young film critics, Caparrós Lera, reports that Herralde's film received a chilly response from an indifferent public.[7]

Although Spanish directors had begun efforts to compile collective memoirs of the Civil War before the dictator's death, they received little cooperation from their national film archives. Thus they have assumed the journalist's chores of taking interviews and preparing montages of their national past. Some, such as Juan Antonio Bardem, prefer fictionalized reconstructions rather than documentary as a means of dramatizing important events. Taking his title from John Reed's *Ten Days that Shook the World,* this still active pioneer of postwar Spanish film recreates an event that emerged from the polarized society that was Franco's legacy.

*Siete días de enero* (*Seven Days in January*) (1979) is an account of the "tragic week," January 25–31, 1976, when five labor lawyers were murdered by right-wing terrorists in an office building near Madrid's Atocha Station. Bardem, with the help of journalist Gregorio Morán, reporter for a Madrid newspaper, based his script on a strict chronological account of the murders. Interspersed within the reenactment of the known facts of the case are fictionalized scenes of the characters' social and family life— an archaic, militaristic sociopolitical context that fosters and encourages armed terrorism. In keeping with a documentary style, Bardem uses unknown actors and scrupulously strives for historical accuracy.

*Siete días* closes on a positive note. A printed message informs viewers that six months after the murders, Spanish elections were held in which no member of any ultraconservative political group obtained a seat in parliament by popular vote. Thus the five lawyers brutally shot down while assisting transport workers in their efforts to strike and gain better working conditions are seen to be vindicated by the establishment of a democratic regime and of a historic new direction in Spain.

Documentary films were new to postwar Spanish directors, who had been prohibited from making any on controversial topics by Franco's censors. Now that censorship had been relaxed, directors could either compile their own documentaries from interviews or footage from outside Spain, as Patino and Jaime Chávarri had done, or reconstruct a fictional account of historical incidents, as Bardem did in *Siete días,* as a way to open up the collective memory of Spain's past. Most directors continued Saura's example of the film metaphor, although, in the transition period, it was no longer a necessity. Among the most scandalous of the metaphorical films of transition is Manuel Gutiérrez Aragón's *Camada negra* (*Black Brood*), winner of the 1977 Berlin Film Festival's award for best director.

Like Saura, Gutiérrez focuses upon the family unit as formative matrix of the fascist mind. In *Camada negra,* the family is seen much as Franco himself had posed it in *Raza;* that is, a small unit or "cell" of loyal fascists whose cult of discipline and sacrifice is dedicated to patriotism and honor. Franco, it goes without saying, paid exaggerated tribute to these values, while Manuel Gutiérrez finds them distorted and decadent. The fascist family of the transition is not the military one of *Raza* nor the wealthy bourgeois one of *Siete días* or *El desencanto.* It is, instead, a "black brood" of circumstances considerably reduced from those of the immediate postwar years, in which supporters of Franco won the spoils of the Civil War, the only jobs to be had, and were able to pay for the food, goods, and housing available to others only on the black market.

The "black brood" is headed by Blanca (María Luis Ponte), a fanatic who dreams of her first husband, a member of the Spanish fascist Falangist party. She lives with her three sons in a vacant state laboratory where she once worked as a janitor. Her sons—José (Joaquín Hinajosa), Ramiro, and Tatín (José Luis Alonso)—are being brought up as terrorists to make destructive raids on bookstores and art galleries. The fifteen-year-old Tatín is under age so is not included in the group, but he wants desperately to be a hero. So Tatín sets about proving himself worthy of the three vows to which the fascist group has sworn allegiance: secrecy, vengeance, and, if need be, sacrifice of anything to the "cause."

The group carries out its violent deeds without the slightest hope of ever obtaining power. Calling themselves the Apostolic Anti-Communist Alliance of Spain (a reference to the Triple A terrorist group in Argentina), the young hoodlums train rigorously. They plan for destruction with pseudoscientific accuracy, trying to determine, for example, the temperature at which paper burns.

One day Tatín meets Rosa, played by the talented young Spanish actress Angela Molina. She is uneducated but enthusiastic and in love with him. In a mad ritual of repressed sexual frenzy and loyalty to his brotherhood, Tatín beats Rosa to death with a rock, muttering, "España, España, España." Thus he destroys the only person who really loved him to prove himself faithful to his family's vows.

Subtle references to Spain's past are part of the fabric of *Camada negra*. Since the Civil War is viewed by many historians as a testing ground that Hitler and Mussolini used to perfect their weaponry for a wider conflict, Gutiérrez Aragón chooses a laboratory, now abandoned, as the family nest. The vows of vengeance and secrecy reflect the repression of the immediate post–Civil War years in which Franco systematically and silently killed thousands of political prisoners. The group's targets are centers of culture, recalling the strong anti-intellectual attitudes and slogans of Spanish fascists, such as "muera la inteligencia" (Death to intelligence) used to shout down Miguel de Unamuno, rector of the University of Salamanca.

Before it won the Berlin Festival Award, this fable had not been released in Spain, apparently through the caution of the Spanish transitional government, which wanted to observe its reception in Germany before allowing it to reach the Spanish public. The year before, 1976, a historical film chronicle of the Franco era planned by veteran film producer Eduardo Manzanos was prohibited by an administration that claimed to have abolished censorship. Manzanos's film was to have been entitled *España debe saber* (*Spain Should Know*), and was to include open discussions of some of Spain's most guarded secrets—the death of García Lorca, Franco's relationship with Hitler and with the Spanish monarchy, and the 1973 assassination of Franco's closest and most faithful ally, Carrero Blanco. The fate of *España debe saber* is still unknown.

Although officially abolished, censorship did not disappear from Spain. Critic and director Antonio del Amo points out that, while eroticism can be dealt with freely, two topics—the military and the monarchy—remain "untouchable."[8] Director Pilar Miró's experience illustrates just how far Spanish censorship is still enforced on the topic of military justice.

Pilar Miró, a veteran television director and former student of law and journalism, is one of the few female cinema directors in Spain. Her first film, *La petición* (*The Engagement Party*) (1976), based on a Zola short story, was banned outright because of its treatment of sadism in the death of a young girl in a sex orgy with three men. The film was released only after the press began to discuss it in public and other directors gave critiques of it. In January 1979, Pilar Miró accepted producer Alfredo

Matas's offer to film an event that took place in the rural province of Cuenca. It was here in 1913 that a local political boss brought false murder charges against two anarchists. After being tortured by police, the two confessed to crimes they did not commit and spent eleven years in jail before being freed in 1924 for good behavior. Two years later the "victim" they were supposed to have murdered, a mental retardate called El Cepa, wandered back into the village. The court denounced the confessions extracted by torture and pronounced "error of justice."

*El crimen en Cuenca* was withheld when an army official protested the public release of torture scenes. During the year 1978–1979, Amnesty International reported fourteen proven incidences of torture in Spain. In spite of official charges brought against the director and producer, *El crimen en Cuenca* was invited to the 1980 Berlin Film Festival. But the impasse continued until a military coup rocked the Spanish government on February 23, 1981. The coup so tarnished the military establishment that the government felt safe in releasing the film on August 13, 1981, two years after its completion. It was an instant financial success. Within three years, in 1984, director Pilar Miró was named head of the Departamento de Cinematografía y Teatro.

The still considerable influence of the military on the Spanish film industry is confirmed by the fact that, while *El crimen en Cuenca* was delayed for two years, Saura's more ambiguous *Los ojos vendados* (*Blindfolded*) (1978) was released without difficulty. Saura's first film after Franco's death is dedicated to his son, who was beaten by a group of right-wing youths. The film also recalls Saura's own experience in which he was invited to attend a symposium on torture by Latin American military regimes. At the symposium he was moved by the testimony of a woman in dark glasses and turned-up collar who told of undergoing torture by a terrorist group.

*Los ojos vendados* follows a pattern in Saura's films in which domestic violence becomes the root of social violence such as war and torture. Emilia, an urban housewife played by Geraldine Chaplin, is beaten by her husband, Manuel (Xavier Elorriaga), who suffers fits of jealousy. Emilia takes refuge with a new acquaintance, her dance instructor, Luis. Luis is also a theater director. He enacts Saura's own experience of having heard testimony by a woman who was tortured. Luis (José Luis Gómez) decides to dramatize the event and chooses Emilia to play the role of the torture victim. The theme thus reverberates on two dimensions, personal and social. Domestic abuse reflects the kind of personal cruelty that engulfs society at large.

The military establishment, not feeling itself threatened by the theme of domestic violence or terrorism, made no objections to *Los ojos vendados*. Yet Saura's film, together with *Siete días* and *El crimen en Cuenca*, expresses the fear of organized violence—whether from terrorists or police—and the tension of Spain's passage from the Franco dictatorship to democracy.

Another theme, infrequent in Spanish film and perhaps another measure of the force of censorship in the transition years, was that of homosexuality. Films dealing with this subject are automatically rated as erotic in Spain, even though they include no erotic images. Examples include the British release *Richard's Things* (1980), starring Liv Ullman, and the Spanish film *El diputado* (*The Deputy*) (1978), both classified in category "S" in spite of the absence of erotic scenes or even nudity. In Eloy de la Iglesia's *El diputado*, a Communist legislator, played by José Sacristán, is found to be gay and is trapped by a scheme exposing his sexual preference and thus ending his career. De la Iglesia responded to the "S" classification of *El diputado* as a form of censorship intended to limit public access and to "protect" a public whose liberty the Spanish government apparently still considers to be only partial.

Thus, Spanish law notwithstanding, censorship of such topics as homosexuality and unfavorable depictions of the military is still enforced in Spain. Since the military looms so large in Spain's past, current official sensitivity toward the topic must necessarily restrain directors dealing with the topic of the Civil War. The metaphorical film style Saura and others elaborated in the postwar period still serves as a kind of insurance against an uncertain transition government unwilling to stress as yet untested democratic institutions. Two films of the transition, both of 1979, illustrate the degree to which ambiguity continues to predominate as the language of political films in Spain.

Manuel Gutiérrez Aragón's *El corazón del bosque* (*Heart of the Forest*) is a political fable by a director who, a Communist for many years, left the Spanish Communist party the day it became legalized. His assessment of Spanish political attitudes is sketched in this tale of Republican soldiers, or maquis, still unrepatriated and living furtive lives as forest guerrillas thirteen years after the Civil War. Juan (Norman Briski), a party member, is sent to seek out the Basque fugitive El Andarín and persuade him to give up his resistance and join the current battle against Franco now being fought in cities by political organizations rather than in forest villages by what have become armed hermits.

As in Borau's *Furtivos,* whose script Gutiérrez Aragón helped write, the pace of *El corazón del bosque* is leisurely. The camera seems distracted from politics by the splendor of the countryside of Asturias and Santander. Based on Joseph Conrad's tale *Heart of Darkness, Corazón del bosque* inquires into the political alternatives of left and right in Spain and finds them both archaic and out of touch with reality. An allegory for Spain itself, *Corazón del bosque* suggests that, after sitting out the middle of the twentieth century in fascist "darkness," Spain faces not so much a transition to democracy as a complete modernization of its political institutions, by now hopelessly irrelevant to postindustrial Europe. This film represents further evidence that the *estética franquista* somehow suits the needs of transitional filmmakers in Spain. As Peter Besas notes, Gutiérrez Aragón makes this film as dense as if censorship were still in force.[9]

Saura, who perfected the *estética franquista*—the aesthetic of repression, as it is often referred to—with his metaphorical film style, continues to elaborate it in the bitter family farce *Mamá cumple cien años* (*Mama Turns One Hundred*) (1979). The family consists of the same characters as in *Ana y los lobos*, minus the military brother, José. The death during filming of José María Prada, whose implacably fanatical face dominated *Ana*, deprived Spanish film of a brilliant comic talent and weakens *Mamá*. Even a completely rewritten script cannot compensate for Prada's absence. For *Mamá* is a vision of Spain unchanging and unchangeable, entirely inconceivable without the overt presence of the authoritarian rigidity personified by the uniformed brother.

The entire family gathers to celebrate Mamá's one hundredth birthday. Mamá is again played by the amazing Rafaela Aparicio. She, like Franco, has lived so long that the family waits desperately for change. The characters who represented Spanish institutions in *Ana* have been modified by the demands of post-Franco democracy. Ana, now married to the scrawny, middle-aged Antonio (Norman Briski), delights in finding everything just as it was during her days as the family governess. Juan (José Vivo), Luchy's sexually obsessed husband, has run away with the maid. Fernando the mystic is now an inventor who can be seen running outside the family home strapped in a hang glider and wearing goggles. Luchy (Charo Soriano), her husband gone and daughters grown, looks forward to the bonanza she will reap by selling the family estate.

Fernando's morbid religiosity has been assumed by Luchy's youngest daughter, Victoria, who inflicts punishment on herself by slamming her finger in a door to make it bleed. At dawn she takes to her bedroom window a glass of water with an egg white in it. Through this cloudy brew, suggestive of murky minds, the camera focuses on Fernando flopping about in his hang glider on the lawn below.

Saura's symbolic space for recollections of the past is the attic. Old objects and clothes delight the family members but also restore memories of childhood jealousies and pain. They dress up in old suits and laugh, but a free-for-all breaks out when the oldest daughter, Natalia (Amparo Muñoz), makes a play for Antonio and he confesses to Ana his infidelity with Natalia the night before. The next morning Luchy, Juan, who has suddenly returned, and Fernando gather on the tennis court to plan

Goya, plate 65 of *Los caprichos*, "Mamá es hidrópica." The visual point of depar-
ture for Saura's *Mamá cumple cien años* (1979). Reprinted with permission from
*Los Caprichos: Franciso Goya*, introduction by Philip Hofer (New York: Dover
Publications, Inc., 1969).

Mamá's birthday surprise: her death. Luchy directs that poison be put into Mamá's medicine. Fernando, though horrified, accedes to the murder plot without protest.

The birthday party is elegant. Mamá is lowered downstairs in her huge armchair. Her dress, like a map of Spain with its provinces, has the names of her various children and grandchildren written on it. An enormous cake is brought and Mamá slurps hot chocolate, smearing it about on her face. When her predictable seizure occurs, Luchy steps forth with her poison. But Mamá, with telepathic premonition, thwarts her children's plot by instructing the faithful Ana to administer her medicine. After his almost half-century dictatorship, jokes Saura, Franco has become Spain itself ruled but not destroyed by the institutions that kept him in power.

While producing a dark farce in which Spain is personified as everlastingly immune to change, Saura treats the characters of *Mamá* lovingly. Even the aging matriarch is found to have special sensory powers. Saura's laughter is chilled by his vision of Spain's future; his characters, however, retain a comic charm. Fernando Fernán Gómez, who plays the character of Fernando, described *Mamá* as an *esperpento*, the bitter comic plays written by Ramón Valle-Inclán which predate by twenty years the theater of the absurd. This term, however, seems more accurately applied to Berlanga's *Nacionales,* a series of three films in which many national types are seen as a gallery of repugnant killers and clowns.

The first of Berlanga's post-Franco farces is *Escopeta nacional (National Shotgun)* (1978), which was inspired by an actual incident. At one of Franco's many hunting parties, his daughter accidentally received a derriere of buckshot discharged by a high-ranking government minister. The hunting party becomes the context for Berlanga's film in which an ambitious and unctuous Barcelona industrialist, portrayed with pinpoint accuracy by José Sazatornil, and his lover arrive at the hunting estate of an aging aristocrat, the marquis of Leguineche, and his son. The marquis is portrayed with the amazing comic talent of Luis Escobar, whose long film and theater career culminates in his consummate *Nacionales* performances. With José Luis López Vásquez as his foolish scion, Berlanga has discovered a richly comic team.

The hunting party is attended by influential figures of Opus Dei, the right-wing lay Catholic organization that exercised extensive political power in the decades of postwar dictatorship. Other satraps of power and wealth, including mistresses and movie stars, complete the degenerate array of influence peddlers at the party. Many of the gags in this highly verbal film are inside jokes based on details of social and political life of the postwar period. But the corruption of power by way of cocktail party wheeling and dealing, crude erotic jokes, and general depravity of the ruling class is elaborated in splendid visual as well as verbal satire.

Using the same leading actors, Berlanga continues to laugh at the idle rich in *Patrimonio nacional* (*National Heritage*) (1980), the second of his *Nacionales* trilogy. Having outlasted Franco, the marquis, who represents the doddering but eternal Spanish aristocracy, and his son José drive their vintage vehicles into Madrid and prepare to resume residence in their mansion, long vacant during the years of the dictatorship. The decaying Linares Palace—at the center of Madrid overlooking the Cibeles fountain and recognizable to almost anyone who has visited the heart of the Spanish capital—was used in the filming and lends a certain authenticity to *Patrimonio nacional.*

The mansion is occupied by another daft matriarch. Like Saura's Mamá, the marquise is huge and bedridden. When her estranged husband, the marquis, arrives, she is decked out in red wig and flaming red kimono. Later in the film she tries to kill him, but the (National?) shotgun misfires and kills her instead.

Where Saura caricatures, Berlanga is grotesque. Juan's wife, Luchy, in *Mamá,* with her harsh features and authoritarian manner, is an intriguing character about whom we would like to know more. In *Patrimonio,* on the other hand, Chus, José's wife, is a one-eyed monster until, about a third of the way into the narrative, she gets facial surgery. Berlanga's fiery Mamá who tries to gun down her husband from her bedroom window is transformed for her funeral by her hypocritical family. They dress her as a nun to lie in state and place a Red Cross suitcase at the foot of her bier.

The last film of the series, *Nacional III* (1983) reduces the anachronistic, opportunistic Leguineche family to a small apartment where they plot how to get their family heirlooms out of democratic Spain. Their country, like France, is now under a socialist government, so they choose Miami as their haven and prepare to move there.

Transition from dictatorship to democracy may have ended with the election of socialist prime minister Felipe González in July 1982. Seven short years, however, cannot begin to dismantle the institutions and attitudes that sustained the dictator and that directors such as Saura pose as Spain's legacy for the future. The films of this period tend to bear out his grim prophecy. The immediate post-Franco years saw directors compiling memoirs from interviews and foreign war footage that at least opened public discussion and debate about the nation's past. Yet, as Spain elected its first liberal government in forty-six years, its film directors seemed already tired of the national past as possible narrative material. Franco's dictatorship lasted so long that, even before it has been thoroughly examined by filmmakers, it has become part of the national folklore—"la religión, las castañuelas, y el franquismo" (religion, castanets, and *franquismo*), in the words of film critic Matías Antolín—and thus is no longer of interest to Spaniards.[10]

Are Spanish directors planning more thorough analyses of their nation's Civil War? "It will be difficult to return to an era of so many years ago," remarked Basilio Martín Patino to this writer on leaving a roundtable discussion of Rossif's *To Die in Madrid* on May 13, 1982, in Madrid. Another young director, José Luis García Sánchez, goes even further to reject cinema treatment of Spain's past.[11]

> *Pienso que hablar hoy del franquismo es claramente reaccionario. Me parece que aquí no ha cambiado nada, que el enemigo es el mismo. Franco es un señor que murió . . . me parece que mirar para atrás cuando tienes tantísima tarea que realizar a tu alrededor y hacia adelante es una actitud reaccionaria . . . Franco no fue el único problema; nunca ha sido él el verdadero problema.*

> (I think that to talk today about *franquismo* is clearly reactionary. It seems to me that nothing has changed here, that the enemy is the same. Franco is a man who died . . . It seems to me that to look back when you have such an abundant task here at hand and in the future is a reactionary attitude . . . Franco was not the only problem; he has never been the only problem.)

Film scholar and critic Román Gubern sees producers cancelling projects that lack public appeal, including "any project that deals with the Civil War, Franquismo, democratic resistance, and the historical memory of Spanish peoples."[12]

> *El diagnóstico de la industria fue que, pasada la inicial curiosidad, el público había decidido olvidar y clausurar su propio e ingrato pasado . . . en consequencia que era menester ofrecer al mercado evasión y euforia, escapismo y optimismo.*

> (The judgment of the industry was that, now that the initial curiosity was over, the public had decided to forget and close its own unpleasant past . . . therefore, it was necessary to offer the market evasion and euphoria, escapism and optimism.)

Saura proved, with *La prima Angélica* in 1973, that fervent national dialogue could be stirred by opening up the collective memory in a popular medium such as film. On screens throughout America and Europe, directors still discover keys to the present in themes of the Second World War almost half a century after the conclusion of the conflict in films such as *Patton* (1970), Lina Wertmuller's *Seven Beauties* (1976), and Syberberg's *Hitler, a Film from Germany* (1977).

Is Spain calling, as did Ana from her balcony, in a whisper so low they cannot hear? Or are the efforts of directors in post-Franco Spain, like Frankenstein, controlled by their producers' economic needs and their own reluctance to open Spain's still unexamined past to an indifferent film public?

The films already made after Franco's death make clear that the history of Spain's Civil War, including questions of social progress and political ideology, remains only tentatively examined in Spanish cinema. Old problems are now compounded by new ones of democracy. As a member of the European Economic Community, Spain will surely be forced to re-examine not only its new economic relationship but wider social issues such as freedom of expression, the role of women in society, and the coming to terms with the national past. Until these themes are dealt with in its cinema, Spain's past will remain unexorcised.

# 11. Conclusion: Franco's Legacy

*Yo . . . era un analfabeto de la temática de nuestra guerra a través de los textos que me inculcaron; empecé a descubrirla con la experiencia de este cine que hago . . .*

(I . . . was illiterate of the themes of our war as presented by the texts they taught us with; I began to discover them with the experience of making this film . . .)                                      —Basilio Martín Patino[1]

Catching up with the past, both economically and culturally, is an enormous task faced by Spanish filmmakers. They must first restructure the industry so as to provide autonomy and freedom of expression, benefits Spanish film has not enjoyed since before the Civil War. The most difficult dilemma will be how to retain state subsidy, which the industry will undoubtedly need for a time, without state control.

Recovering its national past will be no less difficult. One of the legacies of Franco to Spanish film is the aesthetic of repression. This metaphorical, convoluted style, which has become a national genre of postwar cinema, will never reach a large audience in a country in which developments in film remain known only to a small, select group of film students, intellectuals, and an educated minority.

Yet film in Spain plays a more important role than anywhere in Europe. Interviews and surveys about reading habits there confirm that film provides the only source of consistent cultural information for the vast majority of people.[2] So for filmmakers to neglect their national past on the basis that it is not popular inevitably leads to the other legacy of Franco, practiced by the dictator himself; that is, silence about the Spanish conflict and the ensuing era of dictatorship spawned by it.

Because the conditions of postwar dictatorship—most importantly, censorship—endured for so long, Spanish film in the transition period is, culturally and economically, in the stage of development European film experienced after World War II: a weakened industry unable to defend itself from the onslaught of American films or strong enough to quickly build and support a national cinema capable of economic survival in the marketplace. Robert Phillip Kolker calculates that recovery of postwar German and French film required a couple of decades. "It took over twenty years for the West German cinema to reemerge and reexamine itself and its culture. It took the French about ten years to channel the political and philosophical excitement of the postwar years into a renewal of their cinema."[3]

Until the Spanish film industry can reawaken to its past, the most compelling attempt at a truly national cinema remains, ironically, the films of the late *franquista* period. Saura, Fons, Ricardo Franco, and Borau have a sense of national pathos and urgency that seems to have faded as filmmakers adjust to their new freedom. At least one young director, Pedro Almodóvar, has noticed the difference between Spanish film of the late *franquista* period and that of the democratic transition: "Le cinéma sous Franco avait des préoccupations politiques, sociales, il était souvent meilleur qu'aujourd'hui. Il y a une crise de la création, ici comme ailleurs, il y a peu de sujets forts" (Cinema under Franco had political, social preoccupations, it was often better than today. There is a creative crisis, here as elsewhere, there are few overwhelming subjects).[4]

The fact that filmmakers of the transition period in Spain seem to turn away from their national past, especially the Civil War, as compelling subjects prompts reappraisal of Paul Monaco's hypothesis that "a national cinema . . . that has just gone through a collective trauma . . . tends to produce particularly expressive films."[5] Monaco cites Soviet cinema of the twenties and early thirties, American film just after the depression, and Italian neorealism as examples of renewal in national cinema. The fact that Saura's film memoirs and the ironic compilations of Patino and Herralde are as close as Spanish cinema has come to treating its national conflict lends credence to Monaco's suggestion that cinema under stress of national emergency responds with special eloquence.

Now that dictatorship and severe censorship have been over for a decade, recapturing a distant past by a generation of filmmakers who did not participate in the Spanish Civil War will be, as Patino has said, very difficult. If filmmakers agree with their public that it is too late to open old graves, then a chapter of Spain's national experience will be left dark in the popular mind. The film memoirs of Saura, Patino, and Herralde will become national treasures indeed, lone glances at an era as mysterious and unknown by present generations as that of King Tut's Egypt. For films reflect a nation's image of itself. Historians agree, for example, that "for millions of Americans who saw the film during the 1920's, [King Vidor's] *The Big Parade* better represented their mood about the recent war than any number of Hemingway novels or Cummings poems."[6]

Because of the directors of the New Spanish Cinema, including Fons, Saura, Ricardo Franco, Borau, and Erice, it is no longer possible to omit Spain from a thorough discussion of European film. If Spain's most eloquent cinema was produced under the restraints of censorship, it seems certain that today's Spanish filmmakers, enjoying the benefits of working in freedom and change, will meet the challenge of renewing its national cinema. Whether they will demolish the Franco mythology through their own inquiry into their recent past, however, remains an open question. If they do not, those brief metaphors of the *estética franquista* will remain the only film images of an era scripted for Spanish cinema primarily by Franco himself.

# Notes

*Unless otherwise indicated, citations from films are from the sound track. All translations are my own.*

### Preface

1. Fernández Cuenca, *La guerra de España*, II, p. 539.
2. Vizcaíno Casas, *Historia y anécdota*, p. 71.
3. Barthes, *Mythologies*, p. 239.
4. Caparrós Lera, *El cine político*, p. 50.
5. Bofill, *La mujer en España*, p. 56.

### 1. Introduction: Prewar Spanish Film

1. Vizcaíno Casas, *Historia y anécdota*, p. 11.
2. My discussion of Chomón is based on Fernández Cuenca, *Segundo de Chomón*.
3. Caparrós Lera, *El cine político*, p. 38.
4. Utrera, "Eduardo Marquina y el cine," p. 62.
5. García Rayo, "50 años de sonoro español," p. 34.
6. Vizcaíno Casas, *Historia y anécdota*, p. 50.
7. Solé-Tura, *Introducción al régimen político español*, p. 102.
8. Tamames, *Introducción a la economía española*, p. 26.

### 2. Censorship: 1939–1975

1. Gubern and Font, *Un cine para el cadalso*, p. 26.
2. Maqua and Merinero, *Cine español*, p. 243.
3. Gubern and Font, *Un cine para el cadalso*, p. 341.
4. *Primer Plano*, November 3, 1940, n.p.
5. Pérez Dolz Riba, "Situación actual y real," pp. 26–27.
6. Gallo, *Spain under Franco*, p. 307.
7. Galán, *Venturas y desventuras de La prima Angélica*, p. 134.
8. Gubern and Font, *Un cine para el cadalso*, p. 364.

9. Hernández and Revuelta, *Treinta años de cine,* p. 54.

10. Vanaclocha, "Normas e instituciones cinematográficas en España," p. 61.

11. Bawden, *Oxford Companion to Film,* p. 650.

12. *Primer Plano,* March 30, 1941, n.p.

### 3. Early Postwar Film: 1939–1959

1. Souchère, *An Explanation of Spain,* p. 217.

2. *Primer Plano,* November 3, 1940, p. 3.

3. Gubern, *Raza,* p. 14.

4. Unsigned article, *Primer Plano,* August 3, 1941, n.p.

5. Fernández Cuenca, *La guerra de España,* II, p. 538.

6. Mancini, *Struggles of the Italian Film Industry,* p. 112.

7. Egido, "El cine histórico," p. 22.

8. Castro, *El cine español en el banquillo,* p. 91.

9. Torres, "Una película mutilada."

10. Hernández Les and Hidalgo, *El último Austro-Húngaro,* p. 37.

11. Antolín, "Entrevista con Bardem," p. 43.

12. Brasó, *Carlos Saura,* pp. 30–31.

13. Santos Fontenla, *Cine español en la encrucijada,* pp. 14–15.

14. Antolín, "Entrevista con Bardem," p. 52.

15. Vizcaíno Casas, *Historia y anécdota,* p. 127.

### 4. Juan Antonio Bardem

1. Antolín, "Entrevista con Bardem," p. 42.

2. García de Dueñas and Olea, "Bardem, '64," p. 36.

3. Ibid., p. 39.

4. Santos Fontenla, "Contradicciones," p. 16.

### 5. Luis García Berlanga

1. Hernández Les and Hidalgo, *El último Austro-Húngaro,* p. 62. Subsequent citations indicated in the text by page numbers in parentheses.

2. *Positif* 56 (November 1963): 46.

3. *Cinema 2002* 21 (November 1976): 58.

4. Interview with Costanzo Costantini in Berlanga and Azcona, *Tamaño natural,* pp. 182–183.

5. Antolín, "*Tamaño natural,*" p. 37.

6. Escudero, "Crónica de una masturbación," pp. 30–31.

7. Berlanga and Azcona, *Tamaño natural,* p.105. Subsequent citations indicated in the text by page numbers in parentheses.

8. Galán, *Carta abierta a Berlanga,* p. 45.

## 6. Late Postwar Years: 1960–1975

1. McRae, "La filmoteca nacional de España," p. 20.
2. Gubern and Font, *Un cine para el cadalso*, p. 113.
3. García Escudero, *La primera apertura*, p. 85.
4. Antolín, "La Berlinale," p. 41.
5. Munsó Cabús, *El cine de arte y ensayo en España*, p. 18.
6. Torres, *Cine español, años sesenta*, p. 31.
7. García Escudero, *La primera apertura*, p. 196.
8. Pérez Merinero, *Cine español: Algunos materiales por derribo*, p. 36.
9. García Escudero, *Una política para el cine español*, p. 162.
10. Ibid., pp. 197–204.
11. Hernández and Revuelta, *Treinta años de cine*, p. 74.
12. Gubern, *Historia del cine*, II, p. 222.
13. Molina-Foix, *New Cinema in Spain*, p. 22.
14. Gubern and Font, *Un cine para el cadalso*, p. 164.
15. Pérez Merinero, *Cine y control*, pp. 61–62.
16. Rushing, "The Rhetoric of the American Western Myth," p. 18.
17. Vergara, "10,000 dólares por una masacre," p. 118.
18. Mortimore, "Spain," pp. 321–323.

## 7. Luis Buñuel and His Influence

1. Rotellar, Interview with Luis Buñuel, p. 63.
2. Buñuel, "Poesía y cine."
3. Besas, *Behind the Spanish Lens*, p. 51.
4. Patino, *Nueve cartas a Berta*, p. 9.

## 8. Carlos Saura

1. Harguindey, "Entrevista con Carlos Saura," p. 123.
2. Aude, "Le Temps du bunker," p. 57.
3. Kolker, *The Alternating Eye*, p. 380.
4. Morder, "Carlos Saura," p. 78.
5. Saura and Azcona, *La prima Angélica*, p. 66.
6. Harguindey, "Entrevista con Carlos Saura," p. 156.
7. Marinot and Sineux, "Le Temps circulaire," p. 64.
8. Saura, Introduction in *Cría cuervos*, p. 36.
9. Polo, "*Cría cuervos*," p. 54.

## 9. Other Important Directors

1. Paz, *Corriente alterna*, p. 117.
2. Monleón, Review of *Tía Tula*, pp. 7–9.
3. Santos Fontenla, "Camino de destrucción," pp. 7–9.
4. Franco, "Breves notas," p. 103.

5. Vargas Llosa, "Furtivos," p. 81.

6. Ibid.

7. Erice and Fernández Santos, *El espíritu de la colmena,* p. 56.

8. Gillet, in "*Spirit of the Beehive,*" p. 56, suggests that Teresa writes to "some far away, perhaps imaginary lover," while Glaessner, in "*El espíritu de la colmena,*" p. 249, mentions that Teresa may be writing to an adopted child in France.

9. Barthes, *Mythologies,* p. 131.

## 10. Transition: Dictatorship to Democracy, 1975–1980

1. Escudero, "*Canciones,*" pp. 22–23.

2. Antolín, "*La Berlinale,*" p. 38.

3. Jaime Chávarri, *El Pais,* September 9, 1979.

4. Molina-Foix, *New Cinema in Spain,* p. 33.

5. Herralde, "Entrevista," pp. 32–33.

6. Ibid.

7. Caparrós Lera, *El cine político,* p. 117.

8. Marti-Rom and Lajeunesse, "Le Cinéma espagnol après Franco," p. 96.

9. Besas, *Behind the Spanish Lens,* p. 186.

10. Antolín, "Por un cine popular," p. 56.

11. Ibid., pp. 58–59.

12. Gubern, "Cine," in *España sin ir más lejos,* p. 154.

## 11. Conclusion: Franco's Legacy

1. Interview with Matías Antolín in *Cinema 2002* 33 (November 1977): 38.

2. Paranagua, "Le Premier congrès démocratique," p. 47.

3. Kolker, *The Alternating Eye,* p. 130.

4. Quoted by Marti-Rom and Lajeunesse in "Le Cinéma espagnol après Franco," pp. 79–97.

5. Monaco, *Cinema and Society,* p. 139.

6. O'Connor and Jackson, "Introduction," in *American History/American Film,* p. xxiv.

# Bibliography

Alcover, Norberto, and Angel Pérez Gómez. *Hallazgos, falacios y mistificaciones del cine de los setenta*. Bilbao: Ed. Mensajero, 1975.

Amengual, Barthélemy. "La Guerre d'espagne vue par le cinéma." *Positif* 213 (December 1978): 30–36.

Amiel, Mireille. "*La madriguera*: La Pathologie de la bourgeoisie." *Cinéma* 79 (April 1979): 58–59.

Amo, Alvaro del. *Cine y crítica del cine*. Madrid: Taurus, 1970.

———. *Comedia cinematográfica española*. Madrid: Cuadernos para el Diálogo, 1975.

Andrault, Jean-Michel. "A propos de 7 films espagnols." *La Revue du Cinéma* 339 (May 1979): 113–114.

Antolín, Matías. *"La Berlinale."* *Cinema 2002* 39 (May 1978): 36–42.

———. "La crítica y el analfafilmismo." *Cinema 2002* 44 (October 1978): 56–59.

———. "Conozca Ud. su cine: ¡Pan, cine y olé!" *Cinema 2002* 15 (May 1976): 51–55.

———. "Entrevista con Bardem," *Cinema 2002* 44 (October 1978): 40–44.

———. "Por un cine popular." *Cinema 2002* 39 (March 1978): 56.

———. *"Siete días de enero."* *Cinema 2002* 44 (October 1978): 46–47.

———. *"Tamaño natural."* *Cinema 2002* 28 (June 1977): 37.

Aude, Françoise. "Le Temps du bunker." *Positif* 219 (June 1979): 56–57.

Balague, Carlos. "Notas sobre la producción en España." *Dirigido por* 13 (May 1974): 39–40.

Bardem, Juan Antonio. *Calle mayor*. Xalapa, Mexico: Universidad Veracruzana, 1959.

———. *Cómicos*. Barcelona: Aymá, 1964.

———. *Muerte de un ciclista*. Barcelona: Aymá, 1962.

———. *Los segadores*. Xalapa, Mexico: Universidad Veracruzana, 1962.

Barthes, Roland. *Mythologies*. Paris: Editions du Seuil, 1957.

Batalle, Joan, and Domenec Font. "Entrevista con Jaime Camino." *Contracampo* 1 (April 1979): 19–20.

Bawden, Liz-Anne, ed. *The Oxford Companion to Film*. London: Oxford, 1976.

Behar, Henri. *"Cría cuervos* de Saura." *Image et Son* 308 (September 1976): 93–94.

Berlanga, Luis, and Rafael Azcona. *Tamaño natural.* Madrid: Sedmay, 1976.

Besas, Peter. *Behind the Spanish Lens.* Denver: Arden Press, 1985.

Bilbatúa, Miguel. *"Nueve cartas a Berta." Nuestro Cine* 52 (1966): 6–21.

Bofill, M. *La mujer en España.* Madrid: Ed. de Cultura Popular, 1968.

Boyer, Henri. "La Mémoire retrouvée." *Les Cahiers de la Cinémathèque* 21 (January 1977): 125–127.

Brasó, Enrique. *Carlos Saura.* Madrid: Betancor, 1974.

Braucourt, Guy. "Les Coulisses de la tête." *Ecran* 29 (October 1979): 20–32.

Buñuel, Luis. "Poesía y cine." *Nuestro Cine* 66 (October 1967): 20–22.

Caparrós Lera, José María. *El cine de los años setenta.* Pamplona: Ed. Eunsa, 1976.

———. *El cine político visto después del franquismo.* Madrid: Ed. Dopesa, 1978.

———. *El cine republicano 1931–1939.* Barcelona: Ed. Dopesa, 1978.

Carr, Raymond, and Juan Pablo Fuzi Aizpura. *Spain: Dictatorship to Democracy.* London: Allen and Unwin, 1979.

Castro, Antonio. *"Caudillo." Insula* 376 (March 1978): 14.

———. "Cine español, 1976." *Insula* 363 (February 1977): 14.

———. *El cine español en el banquillo.* Valencia: Fernando Torres Ed., 1974.

———. *"La vieja memoria." Insula* 392–393 (August 1979): 26–27.

Cesarabea, Juan. "Once notas sobre el guión de *La busca." Nuestro Cine* 55 (1966): 10–13.

Chevallier, Jacques. *"Las largas vacaciones," Revue du Cinéma* 359 (March 1981): 18–20.

Cirici, Alexander. *La estética del franquismo.* Barcelona: Ed. Gili, 1977.

Cluny, Claude Michel. "La Répétition, ou, L'Espagne punie." *Cinéma 75* 201–202 (September–October 1975): 180–185.

Cluozot, Claire. "Petit planète du jeune cinéma: Espagne." *Cinéma 66* 104 (March 1966): 80–102.

Cobos, Juan. "Entrevista con Berlanga." *Film Ideal* 75 (1961): 14–16.

———. "¿Es posible hacer cine español fuera de España?" *Film Ideal* 77–78 (August 1961): 34–35.

———. *"Plácido." Film Ideal* 84 (November 1961): 19–22.

Codelli, Lorenzo. "Pesaro 77." *Positif* 205 (April 1978): 44–47.

Cornand, André. *"Esprit de la ruche." La Revue de Cinéma* 320–321 (October 1977): 104.

———. *"La Madriguera." La Revue de Cinéma* 338 (June 1979): 194.

Cowie, Peter, ed. *International Film Year.* London: British Film Institute, 1976.

Cros, Jean-Luis, and Jacqueline Lajeunesse. "L'Espagne à Poitiers." *La Revue de Cinéma* 371 (April 1982): 110–113.

Donaire, Concha. "Berlanga, Saura, y Gutiérrez Aragón en 1980." *Dezine* 6 (1980): 4–8.

Dubroux, Daniel. "La Lumière et l'ombre: *L'Esprit de la ruche." Cahiers du Cinéma* 274 (March 1977): 41–44.

Egea, José Luis. "Bardem hoy." *Nuestro Cine* 29 (May 1964): 19–23.

Egido, Luciano G. "El cine histórico español." *Nuestro Cine* 2 (August 1961): 20–23.

———. "Elegía por un cine nonanto." *Insula* 224–225 (July–August 1965): 21.

Equipo Cartelera Turia. *Siete trabajos sobre el cine español.* Valencia: Fernando Torres, 1975.

Erice, Victor. "Responsabilidad y significación: Estética de una crítica nacional." *Nuestro Cine* 15 (December 1962): 8–18.

———. "*Tía Tula.*" *Nuestro Cine* 34 (October 1964): 62–66.

Erice, Victor, and Angel Fernández Santos. "Entrevista con Luis Cuadrado." *Dirigido Por* 13 (May 1974): 32–35.

———. *El espíritu de la colmena.* Madrid: Elías Querejeta Ediciones, 1976.

Escudero, Isabel. "*Canciones para después de una guerra.*" *Cinema 2002* 23 (1977): 22–23.

———. "Cine y cambio democrático." *Cinema 2002* 34 (December 1977): 41–42.

———. "Crónica de una masturbación." *Cinema 2002* 37 (March 1978): 30–31.

———. "Las largas vacaciones." *Cinema 2002* 22 (December 1976): 7–8.

Feito, Alvaro, "*El espíritu de la colmena,* el espíritu de una sociedad." *Cinestudio* 127 (December 1973): 47–48.

Fernández, Carlos. "Cine español: Entre la industria y la administración." *Cinema 2002* 14 (April 1976): 43–51.

Fernández Cuenca, Carlos. *La guerra de España y el cine.* 2 vols. Madrid: Ed. Nacional, 1972.

———. *Segundo de Chomón.* Madrid: Ed. Nacional, 1972.

Fernández Torres, Alberto. "*Siete días de enero.*" *Contracampo* 2 (May 1979): 66.

Font, Domènec. *Del azul al verde: El cine español durante el franquismo.* Barcelona: Ed. Avance, 1976.

Franco, Ricardo. "Breves notas sobre un proceso de trabajo cinematográfico." In Emilio M. Lázaro, ed., *Pascual Duarte.* Madrid: Elías Querejeta Ediciones, 1976.

Galán, Diego. *Carta abierta a Berlanga.* Huelva: Semana de Cine Iberoamericano, 1978.

———. "Luis G. Berlanga, o el cine muerto de hambre." *Dirigido Por* 13 (May 1974): 1–24, 69–71.

———. *Venturas y desventuras de La prima Angélica.* Valencia: Ed. Fernando Torres, 1974.

Gallo, Max. *Spain under Franco: A History.* London: Allen and Unwin, 1973.

García de Dueñas, Jesús, and Pedro Olea. "Bardem, '64." *Nuestro Cine* 29 (May 1964): 24–40.

García Escudero, José María. *La primera apertura: Diario de un director general.* Barcelona: Ed. Planeta, 1978.

———. *Una política para el cine español.* Madrid: Ed. Nacional, 1967.

García Rayo, Antonio. "50 años de sonoro español." *Cinema 2002* 52 (June 1979): 34–39.

Genina, Augusto. "Porqué he realizado *Sin novedad en el Alcázar.*" *Primer Plano,* November 3, 1940, n.p.

Gevaudan, Frantz. "La Cousine Angélique." *Cinéma 74* 188 (June 1974): 72–73.

———. "*Les Yeux bandés.*" *Cinéma 78* 235 (July 1978): 96–98.

Gillet, John. "*Spirit of the Beehive.*" *Sight & Sound* 43 (Winter 1973–74): 56.

Gillisen, Olivier. "*Maman a 100 ans.*" *La Revue de Cinéma* 24 (Supplement, 1979): 258–259.

Glaessner, Verina. "*El espíritu de la colmena*," *Monthly Film Bulletin* 41 (December 1974): 249–250.

González, M. A., and Santiago de Benito. "Entrevista con E. Querejeta y Ricardo Franco." *Cinema 2002* 14 (April 1976): 38–40.

Gortari, Carlos. "Pudor y sensibilidad." *Cinestudio* 125 (October 1973): 32–36.

Grupo Anónimo de Productores Cinematográficos Españoles. "Puntos fundamentales del cine español." *Nuestro Cine* 15 (December 1962): 25–26.

Guarner, José Luis. *30 años de cine*. Barcelona: Ed. Kairos, 1971.

Gubern, Román. *Carlos Saura*. Barcelona: Salvat, 1973.

———. *Historia del cine*. 2 vols. Barcelona: Ed. Lumen, 1971, 1974.

———. "Max Aub en el cine." *Insula* 320–321 (August 1973): 11.

———. "La prehistoria del NCE." *Nuestro Cine* 64 (August 1967): 15–22.

Gubern, Román, and Domènec Font. *Carlos Saura*. Huelva: Festival de Cine Iberoamericano, 1979.

———. "Cine." In Luis Carandell, ed., *España sin ir más lejos*. Barcelona: Ed. Laia, 1982.

———. *Un cine para el cadalso*. Barcelona: Ed. Euros, 1975.

———. "Les Rapports entre le cinéma mussolinien et le cinéma franquiste." *Risorgimento* 3 (1981–82): 197–203.

———. *Raza (Un sueño del general)*. Madrid: Ed. 99, 1977.

———. "Survey of Spanish Film: Trends, Problems, and Genres in Post-Franco Cinema, 1975–1981." *Quarterly Review of Film Studies* 8 (Spring 1983): 15–23.

Harguindey, Angel S. "Entrevista con Carlos Saura." In Carlos Saura, *Cría cuervos*. Madrid: Ed. Elías Querejeta, 1975.

———. "Los ojos vendados: Una denuncia contra la tortura." *El País*, May 14, 1978, pp. 1, 6, 8.

Heredero, Carlos F. "Reflección sobre el transcurso del tiempo en clave de representación." *Cinema 2002* 27 (May 1977): 46–48.

Hernández, Marta. *El aparato ideológico cinematográfico español*. Madrid: Akal Ed., 1976.

———. "Un posible cine alternativo." *Cinema 2002* 11 (January 1976): 44–45.

Hernández, Marta, and Manuel Revuelta. *Treinta años de cine al alcance de todos los españoles*. Madrid: Zero, 1976.

Hernández Les, Juan. "*Camada negra*." *Cinema 2002* 33 (November 1977): 19–21.

———. "*Pascual Duarte*." *Cinema 2002* 1 (July 1976): 29–30.

———. "*Siete días en enero*." *Cinema 2002* 51 (May 1979): 18–19.

Hernández Les, Juan, and Manuel Hidalgo. *El último Austro-Húngaro: Conversaciones con Berlanga*. Barcelona: Ed. Anagrama, 1981.

Herralde, Gonzálo. "Entrevista." *Cinema 2002* 33 (November 1977): 32–33.

Hidalgo, Manuel. *Carlos Saura*. Madrid: Ediciones J C, 1981.

———. "El cine sobre la guerra civil durante los últimos años de Franco." *Cinema 2002* 43 (1978): 31–35.

Jeancolas, Jean Pierre. "Planète espagne: Il y a toujours des Pyrénées." *Positif* 304 (June 1986): 28–36.

Jolly-Monge, Daniel. "L'Anti-vie . . ." *L'Avant Scène,* October 15, 1978, p. 4.
Jorbá, Rafael Miret. "Carlos Saura." *Dirigido Por* 32 (April 1976): 1–11.
Jordan, Isabell. "La Couleur de la rêve: *Esprit de la ruche.*" *Positif* 190 (February 1977): 60–61.
Kinder, Marsha, "Carlos Saura: The Political Development of Individual Consciousness." *Film Quarterly* 32 (Spring 1979): 14–26.
Kolker, Robert Phillip. *The Alternating Eye.* New York: Oxford University Press, 1983.
Kovács, Katherine S. "Background on New Spanish Cinema." *Quarterly Review of Film Studies* 8 (Spring 1983): 1–6.
Labre, Chantal. "Un rituel de la régression." *Positif* 195–196 (July–August 1977): 105–108.
Larraz, Emmanuel. *El cine español.* Paris: Mason et Cie Ed., 1973.
Lasas, Juan Francisco de. "¿Hay realmente un NCE?" *Nuestro Cine* 64 (August 1967): 24–28.
López García, Victoriano. *Chequeo al cine español.* Madrid: Gráficos Casaló, 1972.
Mancini, Elaine. *Struggles of the Italian Film Industry during Fascism.* Ann Arbor: UMI Research Press, 1985.
Maqua, Javier, and Carlos Pérez Merinero. *Cine español, ida y vuelta.* Valencia: Fernando Torres, 1976.
Marías, Miguel. "José Luis Borau, el francotirador responsable." *Dirigido Por* 26 (September 1975): 20–25.
———. "*Raza, espíritu de Franco,*" *Dirigido Por* 50 (January 1978): 62–63.
Marinot, Hélène, and Michel Sineux. "Le Temps circulaire." *Positif* 185 (September 1976): 64–65.
Mariu, François. "*La Cousin Angélique.*" *Image et Son* 290 (November 1974): 114–115.
Martí, Octavio. "*La trastienda.*" *Dirigido Por* 32 (April 1976): 34–35.
———. "¿Nuestro cine español?" *Dirigido Por* 13 (May 1974): 36–38.
Martínez León, Jesús. "*Nueve cartas a Berta.*" *Film Ideal* 192 (August 1966): 343–344.
Martínez Torres, Augusto, and Manuel Pérez Estremera. "Revisión crítica del llamado 'Nuevo cine español.'" *Cuadernos Hispanoamericanos* 234 (June 1969): 748–762.
Marti-Rom, J-R. "L'Affaire du film *Le crime de Cuenca* (ou les résidus du franquisme)." *La Revue du Cinéma* 369 (February 1982): 60–63.
Marti-Rom, J-R., and Jacqueline Lajeunesse. "Le Cinéma espagnol après Franco: De la politisation au désenchantement." *La Revue du Cinéma* 361 (May 1981): 79–97.
Maupin, Françoise. "*Les Yeux bandés.*" *La Revue du Cinéma* 330 (July–August 1978): 132–133.
McRae, William E. "La filmoteca nacional de España." *Journal of the University Film Association* 31 (Summer 1979): 19–29.
Mellen, Joan. "Fascism in the Contemporary Film." *Film Quarterly* 24 (Summer 1971): 2–19.

Méndez-Leite, Fernando. *Historia del cine español*. Madrid: Ed. Rialp, 1965.

Molina-Foix, Vicente. "El cine de la distancia." In Carlos Saura, *Cría cuervos*. Madrid: Ed. Querejeta, 1975.

———. *New Cinema in Spain*. London: British Film Institute, 1977.

Molina-Foix, Vicente, and Augusto M. Torres. "Una entrevista con Carlos Saura." *Nuestro Cine* 88 (1969): 27–41.

Monaco, Paul. *Cinema and Society: France and Germany during the Twenties*. New York: Elsevier, 1976.

Monleón, José. "El NCE en Venecia." *Nuestro Cine* 56 (1966): 8–9.

———. "*Nueve cartas a Berta*." *Nuestro Cine* 53 (1966): 61–62.

———. Review of *Tía Tula*, *Nuestro Cine* 55 (1966): 7–9.

———. "*Tía Tula*." *Nuestro Cine* 31 (July 1964): 18–20.

Monterde, José Enrique, and Esteve Rambeau. "La guerra de España vista por el cine: Verdades y mentiras." *Cinema 2002* 43 (1978): 26–30.

Morder, Joseph. "Carlos Saura." *La Revue du Cinéma* 338 (April 1974): 67–79.

Mortimore, Roger. "Buñuel, Sáenz de Heredia, and Filmófono." *Sight & Sound* 44 (Summer 1975): 180–182.

———. "Spain." In Peter Cowrie, ed., *International Film Year*. London: British Film Institute, 1976.

———. "Spain: Out of the Past." *Sight & Sound* 43 (Autumn 1974): 199–202.

Muñoz, Irene. "*Ya soy mujer*." *Dirigido Por* 26 (September 1975): 38–39.

Munsó Cabús, Juan. *El cine de arte y ensayo en España*. Barcelona: Ed. Picaso, 1971.

Nacache, Jacqueline. "*Maman a cent ans*: Une crise de liberté." *Cinéma 79* 252 (December 1979): 70–71.

O'Connor, John E., and Martin A. Jackson, eds. *American History/American Film: Interpreting the Hollywood Image*. New York: Unger, 1979.

Oliver, Jos. "Consideraciones sobre *La madriguera*." *Film Ideal* 214–215 (1969): 26–36.

Oms, Marcel. *Carlos Saura*. Paris: Edilig, 1981.

———. "Cinéma espagnol d'aujourd'hui." *Cinéma 77* 223 (July 1977): 8–16.

———. *Juan Antonio Bardem*. Lyon: Serdoc, 1962.

Oms, Marcel, and Lilian Perier. "Le Cinéma espagnol par ceux qui le font. Entretiens avec Bardem, Giménez Rico, Roberto Bodegas, Pedro Olea, Jaime Camino, B. M. Patino." *Cinéma 77* 226 (October 1977): 35–49.

Palá, José María. "Carlos Saura y la sociedad española de 1968." *Film Ideal* 209 (1969): 8–16.

Palá, José María, and Jos Oliver. "Entrevista con Carlos Saura." *Film Ideal* 209 (1969): 17–24.

Palá, José María, and Marcelino Villegas. "NCE visto de fuera." *Film Ideal* 205–207 (1967): 65–80.

Paranagua, Paolo Antonio. "Bibliographie commentée." *Positif* 304 (June 1986): 55–60.

———. "Cinéma espagnol: Passé et présent." *Positif* 304 (June 1986): 37–45.

———. "Etudes sur la guerre d'espagne et le cinéma." *Positif* 213 (December 1978): 37–39.

———. "Les Loups et les agneaux: *Maman a cent ans.*" *Positif* 224 (November 1979): 38–45.

———. "Le Premier Congrès démocratique du cinéma espagnol." *Positif* 260 (September 1981): 43–49.

Patino, Basilio Martín. *Nueve cartas a Berta.* Madrid: Ed. Ciencia Nueva, 1968.

———. "*Los ojos vendados.*" *Positif* 208–209 (July–August 1979): 105–107.

Paz, Octavio. *Corriente alterna.* Mexico: Siglo Veintiuno Editores, 1969.

Pere, Michel, "Les Grands Paralytiques à jardin d'enfants." *Positif* 175 (November 1975): 63.

Pérez Besada, Jesús, and Xosé Antonio Ventoso Marino. "El erotismo y la mujer española en el cine durante el franquismo." *Cinema 2002* 29–30 (July–August 1977): 47–53.

Pérez Dolz Riba, Francisco. "Situación actual y real de la economía del cine español." *Film Ideal* 63 (January 1961): 26–27.

Pérez Gómez, Angel A. "Una estética de represión." *Cinestudio* 119 (April 1973): 16–22.

Pérez Gómez, Angel A., and José Luis Martínez Montalban. *Cine español: 1951–1978. Diccionario de directores.* Bilbao: Ed. Mensajero, 1978.

Pérez Lozano, José María. "Bardem: Un cine social." *Film Ideal* 17 (March 1958): 14–15.

———. "*El pisito.*" *Film Ideal* 34–35 (August–September 1959): 34.

Pérez Merinero, Carlos and David. *Cine español: Algunos materiales por derribo.* Madrid: Cuadernos para el Diálogo, 1973.

———. *Cine español: Una reinterpretación.* Barcelona: Anagrama, 1976.

———. *Cine y control.* Madrid: Castellote, 1975.

Pérez Perucha, Julio. *Berlanga, 2: Comunicaciones y debates.* Valencia: Archivo Municipal del Ayuntamiento, 1981.

———. "Dos observaciones sobre el itinerario de Manuel Gutiérrez Aragón." *Contracampo* 7 (December 1979): 23–25.

———. "Mamá cumple 100 años." *Contracampo* 6 (October–November 1979): 71.

———. "Tres años de cine español: La vía Querejeta hacia el posibilismo." *Insula* 327 (February 1979): 14.

Pithon, Remy. "Le Siège de l'Alcazar de Augusto Genina." *Les Cahiers de la Cinémathèque* 21 (January 1977): 48–54.

Polo, Miguel Angel. "*Cría cuervos.*" *Cinema 2002* 5–6 (August 1975): 54–56.

Pozo, Mariano del. *El cine y su crítica.* Pamplona: Ed. Universidad de Navarra, 1970.

Pruneda, José Antonio. "Cine español, 1961: Callejón sin salida." *Film Ideal* 73 (June 1961): 13–15.

Publications de l'Institut d'Etudes Ibériques, ed. *Le Cinéma de Carlos Saura.* Bordeaux: Presses Universitaires de Bordeaux, 1983.

Pulleine, Tim. "*Cría cuervos.*" *Sight & Sound* 47 (Autumn 1978): 260.

Rentero, Juan Carlos. "*Pascual Duarte.*" *Dirigido Por* 33 (May 1976): 37–38.

Riambeau, Esteve. "*Mamá cumple 100 ans.*" *Dirigido Por* 67 (October 1979): 63–64.

Romero, Fausto. "Las nuevas normas de la censura." *Cinema 2002* 1 (May 1975): 35–39.

Roque Arias, María José. "La imagen de la mujer en el cine español." *Cinema 2002* 29–30 (July–August 1977): 54–55.

Rotellar, Manuel. Interview with Luis Buñuel. *Cinema 2002* 3 (January 1977): 63.

Ruiz, Raul. "Relación del feliz estado de la república de Calabuch." *Cinema 2002* 52 (June 1979): 40–41.

Rushing, Janice Hocker. "The Rhetoric of the American Western Myth." *Communication Monographs* 50 (March 1983): 15–25.

Sagastizábal, Javier. *Bardem*. Bilbao: Ayuntamiento de Sestao, 1962.

Sagi, Victor. *Films que nunca veremos*. Barcelona: Aymá, 1978.

San Miguel, Santiago. "El cine español y su nueva etapa." *Nuestro Cine* 15 (December 1962): 2–7.

Santos Fontenla, César. "Camino de destrucción: Reseña de *La busca*." *Nuestro Cine* 55 (1966): 7–9.

———. *Cine español en la encrucijada*. Madrid: Ed. Ciencia Nueva, 1966.

———. "Contradicciones: Notas en torno a la vigencia de Bardem." *Nuestro Cine* 29 (May 1964): 13–18.

———. "Entrevista con Berlanga." *Nuestro Cine* 15 (December 1962): 4–11.

———. "Tiempo de violencia." *Nuestro Cinema* 51 (1966): 12–17.

Saura, Carlos. "L'Album de famille." *L'Avant-Scène*, October 15, 1978, p. 5.

———. *Cría cuervos*. Madrid: Elías Querejeta Editores, 1975.

———. "*Plácido*." *Film Ideal* 84 (November 1961): 24.

Saura, Carlos, and Rafael Azcona. *La prima Angélica*. Madrid: Elías Querejeta Editores, 1976.

Schickel, Richard. "Spanish Films: Paradoxes and Hopes." *Harper's Magazine* (September 1967): 127–129.

Schwartz, Ronald. *Spanish Film Directors, 1950–1985: 21 Profiles*. Metuchen, N.J.: Scarecrow Press, 1986.

Serceau, Daniel. "*Stress*." *La Revue du Cinéma* 370 (March 1982): 41–42.

Silvan, Alfonso. "*La regenta*." *Cinema 2002* 1 (March 1975): 12–13.

Smith, Paul, ed. *The Historian and Film*. Cambridge: Cambridge University Press, 1976.

Solé-Tura, J. *Introducción al régimen político español*. Barcelona: Ed. Ariel, 1972.

Souchère, Elena de la. *An Explanation of Spain*. New York: Random House, 1965.

Tamames, R. *Introducción a la economía española*. Madrid: Alianza, 1970.

Tena, Agustín. "La otra crisis del cine español." *Dezine* 6 (1980): 16–19.

Tena, Jean. "Une génération à la recherche du temps escamoté." *Les Cahiers du Cinémathèque* 21 (January 1977): 120–124.

Torras, Jorge. "J. A. Bardem o la esperanza." In J. A. Bardem, *Cómicos*. Barcelona: Aymá, 1964.

Torres, Augusto M. *Cine de subgéneros*. Valencia: Fernando Torres, 1974.

———. *Cine español, años sesenta*. Barcelona: Anagrama, 1973.

————. "Una película mutilada." *El País,* April 16, 1982.

Utrera, Rafael. "Eduardo Marquina y el cine." *Cinema 2002* 51 (May 1979): 62.

Valleau, Marjorie A. *The Spanish Civil War in American and European Films.* Ann Arbor: UMI Press, 1982.

Vanaclocha, José. "Normas e instituciones cinematográficas en España." In *Siete trabajos de base sobre el cine español.* Valencia: Ed. Fernando Torres, 1975.

Vargas Llosa, Mario. "Furtivos." *Quarterly Review of Film Studies* (Spring 1983): 76–83.

Vergara, Vicente. "10,000 dólares por una masacre (Un estudio sobre el spaghetti-western)." In *Cine español: Cine de subgéneros.* Valencia: Fernando Torres, 1974.

Vizcaino Casas, Fernando. *Diccionario del cine español.* Madrid: Ed. Nacional, 1968.

————. *Historia y anécdota del cine español.* Madrid: Ediciones Adra, 1976.

# Filmography

## Jaime de Armiñán

| 1969 | Carola de día, Carola de noche; La Lola dicen que no vive sola |
|------|------|
| 1971 | Mi querida señorita |
| 1973 | Un casto varón español |
| 1974 | El amor del Capitán Brando |
| 1975 | Jó, papá |
| 1977 | Nunca es tarde |
| 1978 | Al servicio de la mujer española |
| 1980 | El nido |
| 1981 | En septiembre |
| 1984 | Stico |
| 1985 | La hora bruja |

## Juan Antonio Bardem

| 1951 | Esa pareja feliz |
|------|------|
| 1953 | Cómicos |
| 1954 | Felices Pascuas |
| 1955 | Muerte de un ciclista |
| 1956 | Calle mayor |
| 1957 | La venganza |
| 1959 | Sonatas |
| 1960 | A las cinco de la tarde |
| 1962 | Los inocentes |
| 1963 | Nunca pasa nada |
| 1965 | Los pianos mecánicos |
| 1968 | El último día de la guerra |
| 1970 | Varietés |
| 1971 | La isla misteriosa |
| 1972 | La corrupción de Chris Miller |
| 1975 | El poder del deseo |
| 1976 | El puente |
| 1978 | Siete días de enero |
| 1981 | La advertencia |

## Luis García Berlanga

| 1951 | Esa pareja feliz |
|------|------|
| 1952 | Bienvenido, Mr. Marshall |
| 1953 | Novio a la vista |
| 1956 | Calabuch |
| 1957 | Los jueves, milagro |
| 1961 | Plácido |
| 1963 | El verdugo |
| 1967 | La boutique |
| 1969 | ¡Vivan los novios! |
| 1973 | Tamaño natural |
| 1978 | Escopeta nacional |
| 1980 | Patrimonio nacional |
| 1983 | Nacional III |
| 1985 | La vaquilla |

## José Luis Borau

| | |
|---|---|
| 1962 *Capital: Madrid* | 1974 *Furtivos* |
| 1963 *Bellezas de Mallorca; Brandy* | 1979 *La Sabina* |
| 1964 *Crimen de doble filo* | 1984 *Río abajo* |
| 1973 *Hay que matar a B* | |

## Luis Buñuel

| | |
|---|---|
| 1928 *Un Chien andalou* | 1959 *Nazarín* |
| 1930 *L'Age d'or* | 1960 *La Fievre monte à El Pao;* |
| 1932 *Las Hurdes (Tierra sin pan)* | *La joven* |
| 1947 *El gran casino* | 1961 *Viridiana* |
| 1949 *El gran calavera* | 1962 *El angel exterminador* |
| 1950 *Los olvidados* | 1964 *Le journal d'une femme de* |
| 1951 *Susana; La hija del engaño* | *chambre* |
| 1952 *Subida al cielo; Robinson* | 1965 *Simón del desierto* |
| *Crusoe; Una mujer sin amor* | 1967 *Belle de jour* |
| 1953 *La ilusión viaja en tranvía;* | 1969 *La vía láctea* |
| *Él; El bruto* | 1970 *Tristana* |
| 1954 *Cumbres borrascosas* | 1972 *Los discretos encantos de la* |
| 1955 *Ensayo de un crimen: la vida* | *burgesía* |
| *criminal de Archibaldo de la* | 1974 *El fantasma de la libertad* |
| *Cruz; El río y la muerte* | 1977 *Cet obscur objet du désir* |
| 1956 *La mort en ce jardin; Cela* | |
| *s'Appelle L'Aurore* | |

## Jaime Camino

| | |
|---|---|
| 1964 *Los felices 60* | 1973 *Mi profesora particular* |
| 1966 *Mañana será otro día* | 1976 *Las largas vacaciones del 36;* |
| 1968 *España otra vez* | *La vieja memoria* |
| 1969 *Un invierno en Mallorca* | 1980 *La campanada* |
| *(Jurtzenka)* | 1984 *El balcón abierto* |

## Jaime Chávarri

| | |
|---|---|
| 1971 *Pastel de sangre; Estado de* | 1980 *Dedicatoria* |
| *sitio* | 1983 *Bearn* |
| 1974 *Los viajes escolares* | 1984 *Los bicicletas son para el* |
| 1976 *El desencanto* | *verano* |
| 1977 *A un Dios desconocido* | 1985 *El río de oro* |

## Victor Erice

| | |
|---|---|
| 1961 *En la terraza* | 1968 *Al final de la tarde* |
| 1962 *Entrevías, Páginas de un diario* | 1969 *Los desafíos* |
| *perdido* | 1973 *El espíritu de la colmena* |
| 1963 *Los días perdidos* | 1983 *El sur* |

## Angelino Fons

1966  La busca
1968  Cantando a la vida
1970  Fortunata y Jacinta
1972  La primera entrega

1974  La casa; Mi hijo no es lo que parece
1975  De profesión, polígamo

## Ricardo Franco

1970  El desastre de Annual
1976  Pascual Duarte

1978  Los restos del naufragio

## Manuel Gutiérrez Aragón

1969  El último Día de la humanidad
1970  El Cordobés
1973  Habla, mudita
1977  Camada negra; Sonámbulos

1979  El corazón del bosque
1980  Maravillas
1982  Demonios en el jardín
1984  Feroz; La noche más hermosa

## Pilar Miró

1976  La petición
1980  El crimen en Cuenca

1981  Gary Cooper que estás en los cielos
1982  Hablamos esta noche

## Pedro Olea

1962  Ultima página
1963  Parque de juegos
1964  Anabel; Ceremonia secreta
1967  Días de viejo color
1968  Juan y Junior en un mundo diferente
1970  El bosque del lobo
1971  La casa sin fronteras

1973  No es bueno que el hombre esté solo
1974  Tormento
1975  Pim, pam, pum, ¡fuego!
1976  La Corea
1977  Un hombre llamado 'Flor de otoño'
1984  Akelarre

## Miguel Picazo

1964  La tía Tula
1967  Oscuros sueños de agosto
1970  La tierra de los Alvargonzález

1976  El hombre que supo amar; Homenaje a Adriana
1977  Los claros motivos del deseo
1986  Extramuros

## Basilio Martín Patino

1960  Tarde de domingo; El noveno
1961  Torerillos
1965  Nueve cartas a Berta
1969  Del amor y otras soledades

1971  Canciones para después de una guerra
1974  Queridísimos verdugos
1976  Caudillo
1985  Los paraísos perdidos

## Carlos Saura

| | | | |
|---|---|---|---|
| 1957 | *La tarde del domingo* | 1975 | *Cría cuervos* |
| 1958 | *Cuenca* | 1977 | *Elisa, vida mía* |
| 1959 | *Los golfos* | 1978 | *Los ojos vendados* |
| 1963 | *Llanto por un bandido* | 1979 | *Mamá cumple cien años* |
| 1965 | *La caza* | 1980 | *Deprisa, deprisa* |
| 1967 | *Peppermint frappé* | 1981 | *Bodas de sangre; Dulces horas* |
| 1968 | *Stress es tres, tres* | 1982 | *Antonieta* |
| 1969 | *La madriguera* | 1983 | *Carmen* |
| 1970 | *El jardín de las delicias* | 1984 | *Los zancos* |
| 1972 | *Ana y los lobos* | 1985 | *El amor brujo* |
| 1973 | *La prima Angélica* | | |

## Gonzalo Suárez

| | | | |
|---|---|---|---|
| 1967 | *Ditirambo* | 1974 | *La regenta* |
| 1968 | *El extraño caso del Dr. Fausto* | 1976 | *Beatriz* |
| 1969 | *Aoom* | 1977 | *Parranda* |
| 1970 | *Mefistófeles* | 1978 | *Reina Zanahoria* |
| 1972 | *Morbo; Al diablo con amor* | 1983 | *Epílogo* |
| 1973 | *La loba y la paloma* | 1985 | *El año en que murió Franco* |

## Manuel Summers

| | | | |
|---|---|---|---|
| 1963 | *Del rosa al amarillo* | 1970 | *Adiós, cigüeña, adiós* |
| 1964 | *La niña de luto* | 1972 | *El niño es nuestro* |
| 1965 | *El juego de la oca* | 1975 | *Ya soy mujer* |
| 1966 | *Juguetes rotos* | 1976 | *Mi primer pecado* |
| 1967 | *No somos de piedra* | 1978 | *El sexo ataca* |
| 1968 | *¿Porqué te engaña tu marido?* | 1981 | *Angeles gordos* |
| 1969 | *Urtaín, rey de la selva* | 1983 | *To el mundo es güeno* |

# Index

References to illustrations are in boldface type.